THE 75 BIGGEST MYTHS ABOUT COLLEGE ADMISSIONS

Stand Out from the Pack, Avoid Mistakes, and Get into the C...

D1532415

DR. JERRY ISRAEL

FORMER PRESIDENT OF THE UNIVERSITY OF INDIANAPOLIS

SOURCEBOOKS, INC.®
NAPERVILLE, ILLINOIS

Published by Sourcebooks, Inc.
P.O. Box 4410, Naperville, Illinois 60567-4410
(630) 961-3900
Fax: (630) 961-2168
www.sourcebooks.com

Library of Congress Cataloging-in-Publication Data

Israel, Jerry.
  The 75 biggest myths about college admissions : stand out from the pack,
avoid mistakes and get into the college of your dreams / Jerry Israel.
      p. cm.
  1. Universities and colleges—United States—Admission. 2. College applications—United States. I. Title. II. Title: Seventy-five biggest myths about
college admissions.

LB2351.2.I85 2008
378.1'610973—dc22

                              2007045870

              Printed and bound in the United States of America.
                    VP 10 9 8 7 6 5 4 3 2 1

For all those students throughout the years
from whom I learned so much. . .

CONTENTS

About This Book:
A Reader's Guide

What follows is a handbook—a guide, a tool—for high school students in search of a college where they can be admitted and succeed. Parents and others interested in the college search will also find this volume informative.

You will be reviewing 75 common myths about the college application and admission process, as well as the truth behind the myth. I want to share with you what I have learned in my nearly fifty years as student, teacher, dean, and college president to help you make informed decisions in your college search.

The book is organized in a roughly chronological order, from college shopping through the first day of class. However, you are not required to read this book from cover to cover, although you may find it useful to read through the whole book once first and then dip in and out to find relevant information at the right time in the search process.

The 75 myths and the reality for each are summarized in boldface at the beginning of each subsection. They are also organized and connected in chapters based on their relevance to a larger issue of the college search process.

One way to attack the material included might be to thumb through the pages, reading only the introductory statements one after another. If a particular myth seems relevant, timely, or for that matter disturbing, you can then choose to review the explanation that follows. These details become, if you will, almost like footnotes to the myths and realities they explain.

There is little information in this volume that higher education leaders don't know. For whatever reason, however, they have been somewhat reluctant to share much of it with their consumers in the general public. Colleges have a good record to share. Their mission is to help students find their stories to tell. There is no reason not to pull back the curtain and let others in. Enjoy and learn from what follows.

If You Have Time for Just Two Myths, Here They Are

Myth 1: It is a seller's market in which colleges have all the control.

Reality: It is a buyer's market where you have many good choices.

A few brand-name schools can call all their own shots. They get more unsolicited applications than they can even read and basically pick the class they want regardless of the price they charge (which is usually extraordinarily high and far more than needed to educate you). These schools have effectively created the expectation that it is a seller's market. Not true.

There are more than three thousand colleges and universities in the United States. Almost all of them must recruit a substantial number of new students every year. Students come in all shapes and sizes: adult, transfer, part-time, non-credit, and so on. By far the largest subset, and the most desired one, is the eighteen-year-old high school graduate.

Most colleges, whatever else they do, offer undergraduate degree programs. Most colleges have designed their programs for this group. Enrolling a full-time, first-time freshman means having a student who can fit comfortably into the school's model of living and learning, a student for whom few exceptions have to be made, someone who will rent a room and eat the food, who will play on the team or in the band, who will become a successful graduate and lifelong supporter, and from whom, frankly, the most cumulative tuition and fees will be collected.

Graduate students bring prestige to the faculty, but they require close supervision and expensive instruction, research, and library costs. They are often paid modestly to help teach undergrads. They do not produce substantial revenue for an institution. Part-time and adult students almost always pay greatly reduced tuition and fees in order to make it affordable for them to attend. With families and jobs that take up most of their energy, they add very little to the out-of-class life of the campus.

In summary, eighteen- to twenty-two-year-olds pay (or someone pays for them) most of the bills that allow a college to operate and provide most of the vitality that animates and defines the college's culture. Without students, colleges would close. Yet colleges too often act as if they don't understand this simple reality, focusing more attention on the needs of others (e.g., faculty, alumni, and donors). The myth that you as students need colleges more than they need you allows colleges to continue to give you too little attention. If you believe the myth, you are inhibited from acting like a valued customer with questions and expectations.

Remember above all else throughout the college decision-making process that you are a valuable commodity and that it is OK to make schools work to recruit you. When you find a college that acts like it cares, it probably does! Your college experience and the rest of your life will be the better for choosing such a place.

Myth 2: Success in life depends on which college you choose.

Reality: Success in life depends not on which college you go to, but whether you graduate from college!

University officials proudly report that college graduates earn much more money than high school graduates do, and that college graduates have received the tools needed to live a more enriched life. But colleges are less talkative about the fact that half of students who enroll in college don't finish. For students who don't graduate, going to college can be a waste of time and money, maybe even worse than not going at all.

The notion that you must attend one of the brand-name schools to be successful is a function of those schools' excellent reputations and very well-oiled public relations departments. It is more important to choose a college you can enjoy and graduate from successfully than to pick one that, although it has a great reputation, might be a place where you could struggle, be unhappy, run up a large debt, and worst of all, leave without a degree.

You will hear little discussion of the fact that so many entering students never graduate. It is a sad commentary that many colleges have little concern for ensuring that students learn and achieve their goals. Colleges will place blame on high schools for weak preparation or point fingers at students' lack of motivation rather than working to see what they can do to help their students be more successful. A prepared, motivated student will be successful anywhere. Colleges take credit for the achievements of those students even though they probably had little to do with that success. However, many colleges are reluctant to share the blame for students' failures.

The key to good decision making in selecting a college is to search for one that consistently works to make your success its priority. That approach will lead to a true win-win situation for the school and the student. Yet, the college experience is about more than just preparing for life after graduation. The college years are a vital, important part of life itself. To that end, it is important to choose a location and an atmosphere that you enjoy, because where you are happy, you will most likely be more successful in and out of class.

The quality of your fellow classmates and the campus culture they help to create are also vital determinants of likely success. Good students can be role models and mentors as well as lifelong friends and colleagues. This is one area where the high-reputation schools may have a legitimate claim to distinction. Their ability to attract many extraordinarily capable students provides a dynamic academic environment. Inevitably, there is also considerable competition on these campuses for grades and leadership opportunities. In choosing a campus, be sure you have identified at least a critical mass of able students who set a quality tone but without so many as to block your path to getting involved and leading on campus. Involved leaders tend to be successful—and graduate.

MYTHS ABOUT HIGH SCHOOL PERFORMANCE AND STANDARDIZED TESTING

A mother once asked a college admissions director why her son wasn't admitted. "Well, I am sorry to say," the director replied, "your son was in the bottom half of his high school class and that is an absolute standard for being rejected here as decided upon by our faculty committee." "Oh," responded the mother in surprise. "I knew he was not in the top half but I had no idea he was in the bottom half."

Most of us are surely a bit better at interpreting statistics than the mother in question here, but there is still quite a bit of data juggling that colleges do in reviewing your high school record and test scores, as myths 3 through 8 reveal.

Myth 3: Your permanent record of your whole school history impacts a college's admission decision.

Reality: Colleges pay almost no attention to those records, but they do care about your readiness for success and how you are evaluated by your high school counselor.

Parents get sick of, and "educational advisors" make money at, the notion that decisions made when a child is very young will determine or doom the college selection process. To be sure, support and stimulation for a youngster shape much of that person's future. But if a student makes reasonable progress and doesn't become a felon, then his or her records, academic and extracurricular, before the eleventh grade will be required and examined but not scrutinized.

Having A's and B's as a high school freshman and sophomore is surely better than having C's and D's. Taking rigorous academic classes is to your advantage, as are leadership and service experiences. But records for kindergarten through eighth grade are never a factor. Grades in the junior year and the seventh semester of high school are far more important than those that came before. In fact, an argument can be made that improvement in the latter stages of secondary school makes a stronger case for college readiness than a consistent record of achievement. Schools will be looking for motivation and seriousness. With that being said, doing better as college looms closer is a powerful point in a student's favor, although it's not a good tactic to clearly do worse at first just to show improvement later.

Letters of reference generally don't carry much weight in an admission decision either. Admissions offices assume that almost everyone can get a neighbor, clergy person, physician, or employer to say something nice about them. What does matter is your high school guidance or college counselor's opinion. In most high schools, this person can be very important and helpful. Colleges nurture their relationship with key high school counselors. Information and communication flow back and forth. In many cases, counselors have a great deal of experience and longevity in their positions. They take great pride in placing the right students in the right college situations. Families and the college communities know when good placements have been made and when they have not.

Get to know your school's college counselors and work closely together. Seek their advice every step of the way in your search and decision-making process. Feel free to ask them what you can do to help yourself and what they can do for you. Most of all, ask your counselor to go above and beyond in being honest with you and in providing succinct, powerful information about you to their colleagues in the admissions offices of the colleges you are considering attending.

Myth 4: Your performance on standardized entrance tests is all-important.

Reality: There is a substantial debate within the academic community about the value of SAT and ACT tests.

Yes, almost all colleges will require some sort of standardized entrance test. There are two tests you should know about, commonly known as the SAT and the ACT. You can take both, but most students take just one. Which one you sign up for will be determined mostly by what state you live in while in high school and the states of the schools to which you are applying. Both tests are the product of large, important national educational organizations that exert substantial influence over how colleges and students think and act.

The SAT tends to be more common in the eastern part of the United States. The ACT takes over in popularity as you move west. Very few students who take the SAT also register for the ACT, but the opposite is not true. Many students who take the ACT also take the SAT, because the majority of the more prestigious schools are in the East. Students, no matter where they live, who are thinking of attending one of these schools, usually want to have SAT data to report.

It is helpful for you to know that these tests are the subject of some of the most heated and controversial debates in all of higher education. Much has been written in the educational community on this subject. College trustees and administrators are not of one mind on the tests' value or even whether they ought to be used.

Many educators and some colleges recognize that a student's performance on one Saturday-morning test shouldn't be taken as seriously as should several years of day-in and day-out performance in school. Critics of the tests argue that not all students are able to show their ability to be successful in college in a high-stress environment where time is of the essence.

Still others believe the tests, inevitably, have built-in bias that favors students who have had "typical" backgrounds as compared to those who come from different circumstances (race, religion, family, home schooling, etc.). Increasingly, colleges are reevaluating the use of these tests as accurate measures and considering if, in fact, they want to continue to require students to take them for admission purposes.

Despite the debate, the tests continue to be widely used primarily because they offer easily understood, standardized results that can be measured and compared. This widespread utilization invites still another criticism that the tests play too important a role in the decision-making process for students and colleges alike. It seems inevitable when a standardized test is given great importance that students and teachers structure the priority of what is to be learned based on its value in preparing to score well. Teaching and learning toward the test causes factual, easily testable material to be emphasized over more complex concept-based learning.

The SAT and ACT have done well in responding to all of these concerns. However, you may well discover that some of the colleges you are interested in will have eliminated or deemphasized their use of standardized entrance tests. Still, you will have to take one (or both) since it is likely most of the schools on your list still require them. Just relax in the knowledge that these tests are not the most important factor as to whether you will be admitted.

Myth 5: You must take only the SAT or ACT, as designated by the colleges of your choice.

Reality: Colleges know how to convert SAT and ACT data for comparison purposes. It is a legitimate request to ask them to accept the score from the test you wish to submit.

It is well-known in higher education circles that particular states are either SAT or ACT dominated.

As a rule of thumb, the dividing line is somewhere near ACT's home in Iowa. The eastern states, with the more prestigious, well-known (and more expensive) colleges generally expect students to send them SAT scores. Midwestern schools usually quote ACT scores.

The tests are somewhat different in character, although over the years they have begun to more resemble each other. Neither claims to require any advance subject matter preparation or cramming; however, the many classes and materials available to prepare are generally useful in putting students in the right frame of mind for maximizing their performance.

Both tests attempt to see how ready students are for college as a result of their secondary school preparation. The SAT tends to examine basic mastery in foundation skills such as reading and mathematics. The ACT has a bit more emphasis on subject matter.

SAT scores are reported in 50- to 100-point increments. You will hear talk of an 1800 or 2100 on the SAT. ACT scores vary by single point differentials. So, it is common to hear of 22 or 30, for example, on the ACT. Admissions offices have charts showing the relative conversion of SAT to ACT, and vise versa.

Both tests report scores for each of their sections (e.g., your score on the math section). Some schools or departments look toward these part scores as better indicators than the composite, or total, score. If a student indicates a preference for a major in a science or technology field, a mathematics part score might be closely monitored. A possible major in the arts or humanities might suggest, conversely, that the English subject score is more predictive of collegiate success.

Few students in SAT states take the ACT. High-achieving students in ACT states, who might be applying to more prestigious schools in SAT states as well, often take both tests. If you feel one test fits your learning or test-taking style better than the other, or if you have taken one or the other and don't want to spend the time or money (they are not cheap) to register to take the other test, you should ask a college if it will accept the test you want to submit scores from, even if it is not their standard. A school's willingness to work with you on this will be an early but good indication of their flexibility in cooperating with you as a student.

It is a common although somewhat old-fashioned technique to make students fearful of "flunking out." On every campus, there is some scary faculty member who tells students on day one that the person on their left and right will not succeed. Fear works to a college's benefit because it inhibits a student's willingness to take chances or ask questions. Remember that your success is what the college ought to see as its product and measuring stick. ACT and SAT tests are not used, at the end of the day, to keep you out but rather to gauge the entering class's quality. Don't be afraid to work with the test and the admissions office to your own benefit.

Myth 6: Retaking SAT or ACT tests one or more times has high rewards and high risks.

Reality: Most of the time composite scores will change by less than 10 percent upon retaking.

The best preparation for the ACT or SAT is to take one or two available sample past tests. Put yourself under simulated test-taking conditions and see how you do. Take the sample test well in advance of your actual exam date. That way, if you are genuinely disappointed with your practice performance, you can get some help in the specific areas you need. (Most students will have had experience with a PSAT given earlier in your high school career. It can also serve as a good barometer of your readiness for the SAT itself.)

Note that it is difficult to dramatically increase your score on these tests as a result of courses or other efforts to get better results. Some people retake (and retake) the tests, but experience shows scores don't increase dramatically as a result.

However, it is possible to work with counselors in the admissions office of the colleges you are exploring to improve your score. Use the following rationale: The tests are to measure your ability and background—that is, what have you learned that will make you academically successful in college. At best, a particular test on a particular Saturday is a snapshot of your readiness for college. All sorts of factors may impact your performance. If you take the test a number of times, the best score you record is the indicator of your potential. If your score goes down on a later test, it doesn't mean you don't have the potential demonstrated by the higher score.

The same applies to each of the subparts of the test. You ought to be able to mix and match your best part scores to produce your highest possible composite score. This composite of the composite scores is really the indicator of your maximum potential. Colleges shouldn't really care about your performance on any given Saturday but rather use the test(s) to estimate how well you can do throughout your collegiate career. SAT and ACT companies won't mix and match scores for you, but a college can manually if they wish. You might be able to convince an admissions office to mix and match your best part-scores from different test dates, even though SAT and ACT frown on such a practice.

In reality your high school record over your whole career is a far better measure of your true performance potential. There are many students who are particularly gifted at test taking but might lack the right stuff to take advantage of that gift day-in and day-out. Or perhaps you are the sort of student who may not test well but has the persistence, habits, or drive to overachieve what might be predicted of you.

If your test scores don't look as good as your seventh semester high school grade point average, make sure you point that out to your college admissions officer.

Myth 7: SAT and ACT tests are used primarily by colleges to evaluate your ability.

Reality: The scores of entering students as a whole matter more to colleges than your individual score.

Colleges have very few standardized measures by which to evaluate themselves against each other. The average entering test scores of the freshman class are the most common index used to make claims for quality. These scores are published by most colleges and in many college guidebooks.

It is valuable to see how your scores measure up to those of other students colleges admit. SAT and ACT averages are often marketed aggressively by college public relations offices to set the profile they are looking to present. Colleges wishing to compete for only top students will eagerly use good-but-not-great test scores as a prime criterion to reject applicants. This kind of institution will often have a very competitive student academic culture that may not provide the best learning environment for many applicants.

For those students able and willing to compete with very talented peers, a superheated challenging classroom setting can be extremely productive. Yet, it is almost always the case that these upper-echelon achievers will get a good education wherever they attend, simply because they will demand it.

That ACT and SAT scores of entering classes are used as the principal measure of college quality indicates the lack of any really good measures of what colleges achieve or, put even more directly, what students learn. Colleges know the ability of their students before they start their undergraduate careers but have precious little reliable assessment outcome data of how much value has been added to their graduates four years later. Choosing a college on the basis of the quality of students before they begin their education there is similar to picking a physician on the basis of the health of the doctor's patients before they begin treatment. For most matters, including healthcare, evaluative judgments are based on experience not on actions that come before the performance being measured. Why should this not be the case for colleges as well?

Faculty know, one hopes, what they teach but also have few reliable measurements of what students learn. Given many faculty reward systems based on research and publications, it is a good sign if a college demonstrates at least some value placed on faculty's teaching roles. An even better sign for you as a student is if the college understands that its fundamental mission is your learning. Examination of college promotional materials should easily reveal the kind of mindset at work in the campus culture. Being proud of test scores and faculty publications is to be expected. If those qualities are intentionally connected to the way students learn, that is even better.

Understanding that your ACT or SAT score is just a small piece of the data collected by a college to measure and promote its quality should help relax you about these tests and their significance to your particular admission decision.

Myth 8: Standardized test scores of entering students are always reported 100 percent accurately by colleges.

Reality: Colleges sometimes manipulate data to make their best-quality case.

When colleges report the test scores of their incoming students, it is not uncommon for certain subgroups of students with lower scores to have their test data eliminated from the group being measured. If a college has some kind of restricted admission category where students are accepted conditionally, often with a reduced course load at first, the decision might be made to not include such students' scores when calculating the entering class test average. Leaving these lower scores out makes the numbers look higher, or better. The justification is that the conditionally admitted students are not really a part of the "regular" class until they satisfy whatever they must do to gain full admission status.

Another category excepted from the entering student cohort for test-score purposes may be those admitted in part because of a special talent, perhaps in the arts or athletics. Violinists and quarterbacks, to name just a few, are in high demand. Colleges, even those without special arts or athletic scholarships, may have to work extra hard to recruit students with these or other exceptional skills.

A case can be made by the colleges that such students, by sharing their talents, provide opportunities for many more students to benefit. Colleges with orchestras or football teams need certain students with abilities that may well be in short supply. Other students participate in these programs and have more successful experiences as a result of the achievement of the gifted musician or star player. The entire campus community is often uplifted as spectators as well. Why not then treat exceptional cases outside the usual standard? Certainly not all virtuosos or all-American athletes have subpar test scores, but some might. Thus the case is made for leaving their scores out of the entering class profile.

Policies allowing for such exceptions, while often well intended and justified, do create a potentially slippery slope. Remember, figures don't lie, but college marketing officers might figure. One of the things you will learn in college is how to think critically—but you need this skill before you get there as well!

Once again, the evidence suggests a healthy demystification of the entrance test. Students should not take ACT and SAT tests lightly, but neither should applicants tremble at the thought of those special Saturday mornings. The tests do and should matter. But they are just one more fallible piece of information that goes into creating a student profile.

How colleges use the test scores and how willing they are to work with you about test data, and all other information you present, should help clarify for you how well you will fit into this college's ways of doing business. There are many choices for you, and the most important part of the whole ACT/SAT process may be helping you decide which colleges act toward you and the test in a way that justifies including them on the list of schools you want to seriously explore attending.

Myths about How Colleges Build the Applicant Pool

A Midwestern college representative met a prospective student from Miami. One of the student's first questions was: "Is there much country music in town?" While explaining that country music was available, along with several types of music, the rep downplayed its prevalence a bit, thinking this student must not like country music and feared the Midwestern setting being too "country." "Oh, that's too bad," the student said. "I was planning to move here because I love country music." The rep tried to recover and talk about all the country music concerts in town, but perhaps it was too little too late. The prospective student never enrolled.

Just as you don't know much about colleges when you start your search, they often have only limited information about you as well. Myths 9 through 16 help explain how the process moves along, as colleges build their pool of prospective students and you select those few schools you are interested in learning more about.

Myth 9: Colleges only know what you tell them about you.

Reality: Colleges buy information gleaned from the ACT and SAT databases.

In filling out the application for ACT and SAT tests (probably online these days), you will be asked to provide a whole battery of personal information about your background, experience, and ambitions, plus, of course, all the usual demographic data about who you are.

You will also list schools you are considering applying to, so that your scores can be sent to them directly for your convenience. Thus, it's no surprise when those schools contact you, after all you invited them to do so by listing them on your test application. But for every one of those designated schools, you will receive many more packets from schools you may never have heard of before. There will be viewbooks, applications, and in some cases, letters of acceptance and even scholarship offers from schools you haven't applied to yet. This should begin to tell you that you are in demand, and schools will compete to impress you.

You will discover (as will the post office) that your name and address have become well-known to colleges soon after you sit for the SAT or ACT. The better your academic performance, the more unsolicited stuff you will receive—but just about every high school junior gets many, many packages from colleges, and these days, emails as well. Some students might hear from three hundred colleges within three months of taking the entrance test.

College purchases of student data represent the lion's share of ACT and SAT revenue—far more than from the fees students pay to take the test. Obviously, colleges can buy lists of names sorted by test score or by home address, but the process is far more sophisticated than that. The information you and other students provide can be sliced and diced in so many ways. Colleges can request almost any level of sophistication in the data. They might ask for it to be presented by gender or parental income or proposed major field of study or any other variable or set of variables. The permutations and combinations are endless.

College admissions offices work with high-powered research firms to build projected models of what they want their entering student class to look like statistically. They may have a gender or ethnic imbalance that worries them, so they may build in programs and incentives to stabilize the gender or ethnic mix (being careful, of course, not to do anything that smacks of favoritism on either gender or ethnic lines that might violate equal-opportunity laws). Schools with football programs and engineering programs might worry about being too heavily male. Others with strong academic human-service career emphases (teaching, nursing, social welfare) may find themselves becoming two-thirds female in their student population. Almost all mainstream predominantly white schools are doing all they can legally to attract minority students.

Also of great sensitivity is the financial capacity of student families. Colleges like to present their selection processes as "need blind," claiming to be unaware of who might need lots of financial assistance and who might be a "full pay." ACT/SAT data based on zip code and high school attended is often directly revealing of the socioeconomic status of students. There is much discussion in higher education and government circles about just how blind admission decisions are or should be. Just be aware that colleges may know more about you than you realize, and the information can affect which schools may recruit you heavily.

Myth 10: You must score well on SAT or ACT or have a high grade-point average to have a chance to be admitted.

Reality: You don't have to be a high test scorer or achiever to show up on a college's list of candidates.

Colleges buy thousands of prospective student names. They are willing to spend some time and money to see if they can turn a purchased name into a potential student. You probably won't be always able to figure out why you are attractive to a particular college. Don't worry about it. Enjoy the attention for now (although the phone might start ringing soon, and that can get annoying).

Why might they want to see if you are interested? In part, like in most sales situations, colleges work with an understanding of the law of big numbers. They know the percentage of suspects who will turn into prospects, and it will be small. So the bigger the pool at the top of the funnel, the better off the college figures it will be. As the process unfolds throughout the admission cycle, they will eventually stop bugging you if you don't show some return interest. Their staff time is limited, and they will want to devote most of it to their "hot" prospects. But for now, at the beginning, almost all their contacts are computer generated from the ACT/SAT lists they have purchased.

You might be a student who can increase a lower-than-desired male (or female) enrollment. They may think (sometimes they are wrong) from your name that you are a member of an ethnic minority group in short supply. Or maybe you live in an affluent zip code or have listed a major the college wants to strengthen. Perhaps you come from a high school where the college has had great success.

Most students go to college close to home and usually in their state of residence, where financial incentives are often attractive. As a result, if they judge their student body to be too home grown, colleges might be heavily buying names in adjacent states to increase out-of-state ratios in their entering class.

More recently, colleges have been working with consultants to analyze the qualities and characteristics of their current and former students who have been successful. They may discover that their students who have been successful and graduated might have, for example, attended a large suburban high school or resided in campus housing rather than commuting or played a musical instrument or whatever. Armed with this information, computer programs are readily available to match those predictors of college success with the same characteristics of students in the suspect pool purchased from ACT or SAT. If you are a soccer player who plays in the high school wind ensemble, and the college has identified those as qualities shared by significant numbers of their current and former standout students, you will be flagged as a person of potential high interest at this early stage of the admission cycle.

Myth 11: Colleges expect you to read the promotional mail they send you.

Reality: Marketing consultants educate colleges to the fact that students won't look at promotional mail very long.

Most of the material you receive from colleges will be quite attractive. Much of it will be unsolicited and from schools you likely have never heard of before.

Market research tells colleges that fifteen seconds is all the time you will give their glossy publications before you decide to keep them or toss them away. Every school works to create quality publications with the right pictures and text to start to get you interested. They want their school to stand out from the rest of their competition, who will also be sending you material.

Most schools have carefully designed their marketing programs to send you several pieces phased over designed intervals of time. Creativity abounds. Some colleges cut up and attach pieces of dollar bills or bookstore coupons to cause you to look for their later mail to see if you can find all the parts so you can glue them back together and use them.

What messages a college delivers at this stage of its admission process are very important for you to digest. Obviously, each school wants to put its best foot forward and make a good first impression. Pictures may look casual and collegiate, but rest assured they are managed down to the finest detail. Urban schools will want to show you their attractive array of cultural activities while making you feel secure about the campus and neighborhood. Rural schools will want to show off their acres and acres of practice fields and natural landscapes but also reassure you that there are plenty of fun things to do.

Schools with challenging academic programs will picture engagement in the classroom and the laboratory. Where an active social life or athletic program is perceived as an asset, out-of-class experiences will be front and center. Every school these days includes ethnic minorities and working adult students in their pictures. The percentage of minorities and older adult students pictured probably reflects pretty closely the percentage in the student body. One black student among ten student pictures probably means the school is overwhelmingly white.

Seeing four working adults in a group of ten students usually means the school has a high profile of older adult students.

Materials are designed to send messages, sometimes not so subtle, about the qualities and characteristics of the school and the student body they desire. So it is important to let those images soak in as you scan. Is this the kind of place where you could fit in? Do you see yourself in those same pictures a couple of years down the road?

There is nothing absolute or foolproof about this quick look into the nature of the colleges you are exploring. Much more will be learned later in the all-important campus visits you will take. However, early impressions are important in starting to form opinions. Keep an open mind, but start using what colleges send you to help pick the ones you wish to learn more about.

Myth 12: Colleges wait for you to apply.

Reality: Colleges start building their candidate list long before applications come in.

To get the number of new students a college needs in the fall of year 2010, let's say, admissions faculty know they must start collecting enough names at the top of their applicant funnel eighteen–to twenty-four months earlier, during the 2008–2009 school year. This stage of the recruitment process—acquiring the names and sharing information with high school juniors—is the active beginning for colleges of the recruitment for students who will start in the fall a year later. College admissions offices work with students over an eighteen-month period and are thus always engaged with two years worth of new students at a time. As we have seen, colleges think of the process as a funnel, much, much wider at the top and narrowing all the way to a very small opening at the bottom, which is the actual entering class of first-year students.

If you respond proactively early in the process in any way to a college by writing, calling, emailing, or seeing one of their counselors at your school or at a college fair, you will switch your status from suspect to that of a prospect.

Colleges indeed call this early phase of the recruitment process prospecting. A prospect is more than a name. It represents someone who for whatever reason is judged to have at least some interest in attending that school. Most names never become prospects. The greatest shrinkage in the funnel comes right at the top. You will throw away, or at least not follow up even a little with, most of the schools that have bought your name and sent you materials. Schools will really gear up their approach to you once you become a live prospect. Their goal now will be to increase your interest so that you actually apply for admission.

If colleges are going to try to turn you into a prospect, it is helpful for you to reverse the process on them and do some winnowing yourself. Think about the whole recruitment/selection cycle proactively, just the way colleges do. By knowing their intent (which they are reluctant to explain) you can match up with them better. Your thinking and actions will be well paced with theirs. Your communication will be in sync, timely, and appropriate. Colleges want you ready for them at various stages; they set the deadlines. By understanding their motivation, you can be a more effective shopper and can capture some sense of control over the process yourself.

Starting your search as early as colleges start theirs makes sense. But whenever you begin, build yourself a decision-making calendar. Take whatever time you have available and divide it into three roughly equal periods. Label the first of these (six months if you start in the middle of your junior year in high school) "Prospecting and Visiting," where you will sort schools you seem interested in learning more about and get firsthand information. Call the second phase "Applying for Admission and Financial Aid," and that's what you will do. Finally, the third section is "Deciding and Preparing to Start School," which will take you right up to move-in day and your first classes.

Myth 13: Admission decisions are based on your individual abilities.

Reality: Colleges are trying to sort potential students into a number of categories (e.g., gender, race, academic ability, country of origin, financial resources, intended major, resident or commuter, athlete, musician).

Colleges want a class that is balanced to match their structure and offerings. As we have seen in myth 10, college admissions are affected by a wide variety of program opportunities and concerns. If residence halls are segregated by gender and designed to be divided fifty-fifty, men and women, it will be a problem if three-fourths of all their potential residential applicants are women. Perhaps a school is working to strengthen a particular academic area to be marketed, and your proposed field of study is one where more students are being sought for the immediate future. Or maybe there is a perception that more international students are needed to increase campus diversity.

You should be sorting too. It will be helpful to put the materials you receive (or the websites you visit) into some sort of classification system. Anything that makes sense to you will help get you started and probably reflect your value system, even if you haven't thought it through.

You could start with the distance from home. Like many teenagers, you probably imagine going far, far away. Oddly, the closer students come to making the final decision, the more they rethink wanderlust and elect to stay nearer to home. Four out of five American college students in the past decade chose to attend a school within a two-hour drive of their homes. Even those who elected to attend a school farther away had a much higher than average rate of transferring back to a local school after one or two years away.

You might sort between small, usually private colleges with small classes and big, usually tax-supported state schools with more traditional aspects of college life, such as fraternities and big-time athletics. You might further sort the latter group by those in your state, which will almost always be more affordable, and those out of state, where the cost might be much closer to what a private school will charge.

Other sorting categories might include the following:

- Church related—Do you want to go to a place where spirituality might be openly discussed and encouraged, or does that matter?
- Gender specific—Would you prefer a single-gender college? There are just a few all-male schools left but quite a few all-female.
- Campus life—Do you want a strong fraternity/sorority (Greek) system or maybe none at all?
- Community life—Would you like to be in a big city or in a small town?
- Specific areas of study—do you know for sure what you want to study? Most students either don't or just think they do.

- Alcohol and visitation policies—Is it important to be at a campus where drinking and cohabitation are closely policed, or where they are not?

You can't necessarily answer these questions from the materials sent to you, but you can get a start. By sifting through what you receive, you begin to get a better sense of what schools are telling you they value. You are becoming a more informed consumer. You will probably start to have some questions banging around in your head. It doesn't matter if you sort some schools into the wrong category now. You will doubtless make some mistakes. Some schools might be misplaced and disappear never to return to your active consideration. Sure, they might actually have been great choices for you, but don't sweat it. There is not just one school for you. There are several or even many. You are not trying to find the perfect school, just a very good one that suits you well and where you can be successful.

When you have a number of schools sorted into categories, internal comparisons become easier. Instead of one big clump you have smaller groups to work with: the big city ones, the more than two hours from home ones, and so forth. Next try to begin prioritizing your interest within each group—there is a method to the madness, but don't worry about that yet. At this stage you should be looking for reasons to include, not exclude, schools. There is plenty of time later to find negatives and be critical. This is the time to please mom or dad by including their alma maters, which they have always claimed they weren't trying to influence you toward considering. This is also the time to get out all those guide books that try to rank colleges' strengths and weaknesses, which brings us to our next myth.

Myth 14: The media's ranking of colleges is widely trusted.

Reality: Colleges watch the various magazines and books published about rankings with a wary eye.

You should read the national magazine college rankings with caution. Although authors and editors try to sound scientific, there really are no commonly accepted criteria that all, or even very many, professional university people can agree upon. At first, these highly publicized ratings were purely a beauty or popularity contest. Magazines each year sent a list of schools to presidents, deans, and admissions directors of similar institutions and asked them to rank the quality of all the colleges listed. More recently, this rating system, while still used, only represents about 25 percent of a school's score. Other data is collected that seeks to ferret out a college's quality of faculty and student body, its financial wherewithal, its ability to graduate its students successfully, and so on. Some guidebooks also try to collect a sampling of student attitudes towards their schools.

There is heated debate about the categories selected to be evaluated and even more on the tools used to do the measuring. Naturally, if a college is well ranked, the public-relations team of that institution will take full advantage of the good news. Promoting an institution's high rank seems to have a very positive effect on its market position. Some colleges report as much as a 20 percent increase in applications in a year when their standings have experienced marked jumps up the polls.

Equally predictable, if a school gets a lower evaluation than it expects or has gotten in the past, the college administration, if it says anything, will likely question the validity of the methods used to do the rankings. Some presidents have even written spirited letters to national media sources calling for a major overhaul of the ranking guides now published. Some of the magazines are sponsored by national corporations, and there have been whispers that colleges with whom these corporations are closely linked sometimes seem to do better than expected in the ratings.

Each fall a fresh supply of updated publications is available for your review. It is good to have one or two available as you prospect. Everyone naturally seeks independent validation of important and complex decisions such as choosing a college. But do not take what you will find in the guides as gospel. The rankings cannot reflect all the things about a college that you or any other individual student might value. The schools themselves provide you little impartial evidence to go by since they are all marketing their own competitive advantages.

The guidebooks take on an all-too-central role in the process of selecting schools to get serious about. You can't pick a college from a magazine. But as you are sorting among your prospect schools, taking a look at what a couple of the better-known guidebooks have to say about the schools you are studying will be helpful in causing you to focus some of your thinking.

Myth 15: You may not get into college.

Reality: It is not as difficult to get accepted as colleges would like you to believe.

The notion that it is hard to get into college smacks again of fiction perpetuated by elite colleges. If you do your prospecting carefully and realistically, *you will get in!*

With that being said, it's one thing to be a customer, and it's another to have the resources to make a purchase. Similarly, anyone can think about going to a particular college, but it's another thing to have the attributes to be admitted. So if you're interested in a school, you need to do some analysis on whether you fit what the school is looking for in its students. Guidebooks and counselors can help, or even better just ask the college. Find out what the average test scores and class rank for entering students were last year. See where you fit.

Armed with this information, you have some soul searching to do. Be honest—there's no sense fooling yourself. Where would you do best?

Some students want to be around others who have as much or more ability than they do. These kinds of students want to be challenged to compete. They are like tennis players who only want to play people who are better at the game than they are. They want to be pushed to get better. If this fits your learning style, move the schools with higher academic student profiles toward the top of your stacks. But be careful. If a tennis player is that much better than you, your game might be a very short one with little to be learned except humility. Stretching yourself is good, but keep it within reason.

Or perhaps you are the sort of person who really needs to excel and be noticed for it. There's nothing necessarily wrong with that; it just isn't going to happen very often at really competitive schools. Not everyone can be in the top half or tenth of the class all the time. For this type of learner, perhaps schools with somewhat lower academic profiles might be more in order.

No matter which way you think you lean on this challenge/excellence scale, make sure you leave some flexibility in the kinds of schools you are considering.

You will often hear about students applying to this or that school as their "fall back." The notion seems to be that the set of colleges being considered ought to represent a range of difficulty to be admitted. That way if you apply to one or more schools where you might not be accepted, you can "fall back" on some safe ones to guarantee you will get in somewhere.

It certainly makes sense not to apply to a number of identical schools. You have been sorting to make sure there is variety reflecting your set of values in the schools you are considering, and you may have uncertainties and doubts (who doesn't) in that value set to be sure. However, don't view this variety as a "fall back" into a college. What a dreary way to start such an important part of your life! Rather you are keeping your options open and planning your strategy to stay flexible as long as possible. Remember, you are in control of this phase of your life. Colleges are not.

Myth 16: Colleges are very choosy about who gets admitted.

Reality: They want you as much as or more than you want them.

This is when your sorting and prioritizing pays off. You have several categories of schools and a top couple of places in each set. Now is the time to remember where we started with myth 1—colleges want you! They are eager for you to have them on your short list to visit. Colleges know that most of their entering students will have visited their campus at least once at some point in the decision-making process. You should look upon deciding where to visit also as a key step for you in selecting the school (remember myth 2 as well) where you can be most successful.

What is the ideal size for the list? There isn't any exact formula. Don't make up categories just for the sake of it. You might have two or three subgroups, or you might have six or more. Always be practical and realistic, but this is a stage where you can still afford to be a bit playful too. Generally, it is best to visit one or two schools in each category. Keep in mind that you can always make exceptions. You might have one category, say a single-gender college, where just one school holds any interest for you at all. Fine. Or you might have a group, say tax-supported state universities in your home state, where you can't really separate from among three different places. Also fine.

Set yourself a goal to have a working list that you are willing to share with others, and have it ready by a certain date, say the day of the last final exam of your high school junior year in May. Run the list past your counselor, parents, and friends. Listen to their reactions. Don't overreact, and ask them not to either. This is a shopping list. It is not set in stone. Your folks might get nervous about costs (they probably already are). Counsel them that you know there is a great deal of talk that has to happen yet with the schools about price.

People who care about you will get excited that you have made this much progress on your own. Even if deep down you aren't that excited yourself, try to relax and lean into the summer ahead. You get to window shop, to try on all sorts of new and exciting possibilities without having to make a single decision or spend any money, except for the transportation, to visit a few campuses you now know something about and are eager to learn a whole bunch more.

Turn your list into an itinerary. Fit that schedule into the many other responsibilities and fun you have planned for the summer. Organize the materials you have about each school you will visit. Go on their websites again to familiarize yourself with as much as you can about the physical campus and its people. You are ready.

When you decide which schools you want to visit, call or email them. Let them know what you are considering and ask if they have any way to help with the cost of the trip. Some colleges might have overnight accommodations available or can suggest some at a discounted rate in the area, if you need them. Others might even help with the gas money. There's nothing to lose here.

Push self-doubts and second thoughts as much as possible to the back of your mind. You have finished the vital first phase of your search. Now go visit.

MYTHS ABOUT THE CAMPUS VISIT

Look over the shoulder of an admissions counselor for a Midwestern college:

"While I feel like I've had every type of scenario in my office, including a young man who began vomiting in the middle of our meeting, perhaps one of my most interesting was when a family set up their video camera in the corner of my office. They said they wanted to make sure they remembered everything I was telling them about the university and, therefore, wanted to tape our conversation. Talk about nerve wracking!"

Surely your visit will be a good deal more fun than that for all concerned. Myths 17 through 23 will get you ready to make the most out of your time on the campuses you want to get to know much better.

Myth 17: How pretty a campus looks tells a great deal about its quality.

Reality: Some campuses like to build expensive monuments, gardens, and front doors in order to impress you and others.

If you need accommodations from the college you are visiting, you might want to let them know you are planning to be there. Otherwise, here's a rule of thumb: Surprise them, arrive unannounced. This first visit is not—repeat, is not—to decide where you want to enroll. Your purpose is to gather firsthand impressions to help you decide where you will apply and to begin to build relationships with campus people. (Try if at all possible to not visit alone. Parents, siblings, and friends make good scouting-party alter egos.)

You will need to revisit the school at least once as you get closer to a decision. For that visit, of course, you will work out a schedule in advance to include classes, appointments, activities, and an overnight stay.

For this first visit, see how well the school can scramble. This is a quality that will come in handy for you when you are a student there and also tells you how agile they want to be. How prepared are they for any eventuality? How flexible and customer-friendly can they be when not expecting you? They know you from their database (remember they have your name and sent you a bunch of stuff). Chances are, you have responded to something they sent if they are on your list. That means you are on theirs, and they should be able to quickly give you personalized attention.

If you can work it out, take some time to scope out the campus by car and on foot before you announce yourself at the admissions reception areas. This will give you a flavor of the place. How is the signage? Is there any? Has the institution taken the time and effort to make itself hospitable? Is the campus pedestrian-friendly? What about parking? If it's summer, the campus won't be very crowded, but are the lots convenient and cared for?

Pay special attention to maintenance of the facilities. The physical appearance is important to gauge the degree of thought that goes into the campus' effort to make a first impression. Is the trash picked up? Remember that on some campuses there may be an intent to not be too spic and span. A little studied shabbiness, like threadbare patches on a faculty member's jacket sleeve, is often a part of the charm, especially of an older campus. But things falling apart or down, what colleges call deferred maintenance, are a danger signal either of a lack of care or a lack of money. Universities have to pay their people, and they are very labor-intensive places that require large payroll expenditures even though individual salaries are often not that large. It will take some digging (although it can and should be done) to obtain and decipher financial statements. But broken things that haven't been fixed is a worry. Will the school be able to provide you with the best programs and people if there aren't enough dollars to go around?

Myth 18: You can get the same experience pretty much everywhere.

Reality: Each school has its own culture.

Try to stop by a campus snack shop or something like it to debrief with your visit partners. Weigh what you are observing on campus against the materials on the school that you've seen before. Soak up the social atmosphere; you will spend so much of your time eating and talking once you are a student. The campus atmosphere during summer is different, but things can still be gleaned. How do campus folks interact with each other?

The physical design and layout of the campus has not happened by accident. Colleges work with architects and design teams who specialize in campus architecture. What have they chosen to put front and center probably represents what they hold most dear.

Is the bookstore easy to find and user-friendly? Are there books of interest for sale or just text books and T-shirts? Does the library sit at or near the hub of the campus? The answers to those question can signal a vital, dynamic academic culture, or just the opposite.

Does the student center, the heart of out-of-class activities, appear to provide ample one-stop shopping for services such as career exploration, healthcare, and student government? If so, that suggests a robust on-campus student residential population that makes use of the facility actively.

If fraternity/sorority life is important to you, do you see an array of well-maintained Greek houses? If athletics or intramural recreation matters in your search, check out how courts, fields, and pools are maintained.

College cultures are very hard to change and have impacted much of what you see. Is the bookstore open nights and weekends? Does it have space to hang out and read? Are their racks of magazines to browse? The hours certain services are available is a great indicator of use and priority. Things that close at the end of the nine-to-five business day aren't of much value to residential or part-time evening students.

Are religious symbols displayed? Colleges with strong church ties will almost certainly represent their spiritual relationships clearly.

Take a good look at what the faculty and staff wear. Dress codes have relaxed dramatically on campuses in the recent past. Jackets and ties, especially in the summer, reflect an institution that may well be traditional and conservative. Blue jeans, ponytails, and pets on campus are signals of a school welcoming unconventional lifestyles.

Most colleges will fall into a fairly similar and safe pattern, not too risky, not too staid. However, there are campus cultures that cater to almost every taste or standard. If a particular value is important to you, a few hours on campus and some careful looking around will tell you how comfortable you might be.

When you do your campus tour with a current student, the hunches you have about what's "in" and what's "out" on campus can be probed in-depth. You will find current students remarkably forthcoming about such things.

It makes sense, if possible, to visit a few campuses close to each other. If the schools are near to each other, it saves on travel time and expense. Plus there is a value to seeing quick comparisons. On the other hand, you can get burned out if you try to cram all your visits into the same whirlwind trip. So, given all the demands of time on you and family or friends, use a good bit of the summer to get them all done. If there is break in time between earlier and later visits, make sure to get some notes written up after the first trip(s). Photos taken will be useful to jog your memory. If you enjoy putting scrapbooks together with these pictures and other items collected, that would be great.

Myth 19: There's always a clear advantage in being at a small campuses.

Reality: Small colleges provide a homey environment, but also like to know your business.

Most college offices close fairly early in the quieter summer time. Arrive at the admissions reception area with at least a few hours to go in the day. Don't be shocked if they aren't surprised to see you. A sharp-eyed campus person may have already spotted you out and about on campus—a high school senior and guests stick out pretty easily. In some particularly friendly places, someone may approach you before you get to announce yourself and your presence. That's OK. If that happens, how does it feel? Do you like being noticed? Or would you rather be anonymous when you want to be? That's important to know because it begins to tell you how life on campus will be day-to-day and how comfortable you are going to be there.

Years ago, colleges, especially small ones, intentionally tried to play a parental role. They spoke of being "en loco parentis," or serving in place of the parents. There were curfews and rigid social rules. This posture has certainly relaxed over time, but the character of these colleges still retains a nurturing, somewhat protective quality.

It is not uncommon on small college campuses, where everyone knows almost everyone else, for problems to be noticed quickly. Students missing several classes in a row may receive a concerned call from a dean of students. Student residence hall assistants are trained to identify issues their classmates may be facing, whether it is homesickness, partying, relationship breakups, or academic difficulties.

Small colleges provide a safety net that makes it hard for students to fall through the cracks or hide easily. You need to measure for yourself the advantages (people will know your name and you will get help with your concerns) against the disadvantages of a hot-house environment where privacy will be hard to find.

Large universities, most with graduate and professional programs, recruit faculty with the promise of distinguished research and publication careers. These faculty members can introduce students to the cutting edge in their respective fields. Since there are fewer rewards for excellence in teaching at these "publish or perish" places, it may be difficult for the average undergraduate to have much direct faculty contact. A good deal of instruction is provided by teaching assistants, who are graduate students working to help pay for their own education. Such TAs are frequently the butt of jokes about bad teaching, but they may in fact be qualified and able to relate, because of their age, to their younger students.

On a small college campus, faculty rewards are usually less tied to research and more directly related to teaching. At most of these schools, faculty contact for students is much easier. Yet, these faculty members may not be able to share the same kind of state-of-the-art perspective on their scholarly fields.

A visit can help you determine whether you fit best at a small school or a big college. These are the sort of issues campus visits begin to help clarify if you keep your eyes open and ask good questions.

Myth 20: You are the one being evaluated during the visit.

Reality: You have lots of choices, and colleges know it.

There will be a little stress in your visit because you want to make a good impression, but here is where you must remember the central premise of the most important myths again: Colleges need you as much as, or more than, you need them. They will or at least should be selling to you, that is, trying to convince you to be interested in their programs.

Be alert. How friendly is the first person you encounter? This could be a staff member or a current student working for the summer. Are they put off by your lack of an appointment? How willing are they to accommodate your drop-in? Do they want to send you away by making an appointment for another day?

Just tell the truth and be courteous and direct. Let them know, if it seems appropriate, that you wanted to drop in when they were not expecting you. By doing this, you establish yourself as a person who is thoughtful and gutsy. Most of all, you have begun to rebalance the relationship about whose decision this will be. Of course, the college can decide if it wants you, but so too, you can decide about them. The people you will be dealing with know you have lots of choices—if they don't or don't want to admit that fact, you should probably think twice about applying and studying there. It is good to let them know nicely that you are an aware shopper. They should respect you for that insight. Of course, you will do all this in a pleasant not pushy manner, so they know that you are not only well informed but also well mannered.

After some initial getting acquainted, establish

that you are deciding where to apply (they will probably ask). Let them know that you have done your homework and that they are on your reasonably short list. Thank them for the information they have sent. Try to mention a fact or two that you remember. This will certify that you are serious and will impress them. The school has devoted much time and money to developing useful, attractive marketing materials, and they appreciate the feedback. Don't be afraid to tell them nicely what you didn't find useful as well.

You and the person(s) you are talking to should establish what can be accomplished with the time you and they have available. You want two things most of all: a campus tour with a student ambassador and a few minutes with at least one relatively senior admissions staff member.

Watch the way staff members and students relate to one another. Is there a relaxed, comfortable rapport? Does there seem to be a smooth-running process of handling your requests and the others that they are managing at the same time? An admissions office is the sales arm of a university and should be structured in an intelligent manner to put the school's best foot forward. If the leadership doesn't value its admission systems, it doesn't bode well for their other priorities, or yours, as well.

Myth 21: The students you meet on tour are typical of the college.

Reality: Tour guides are chosen because they embody and reflect the characteristics the school wants to promote.

Part of the reason for scoping out the campus before the tour is so that you don't have to pay too much attention to what you are seeing while you walk with your student tour guide. You want to devote your full attention to this student. This is your first, best opportunity to measure what it takes to be successful here.

If your visit is a "drop-in," you might get potluck with the tour guide. If they know you are coming, they may very well try to pair you with a student of similar interests or background. But don't sweat the choice of your student ambassador either way; he or she (women seem to be better students these days and more willing to do this sort of thing) will not be a random selection. Those students invited to be ambassadors, especially in the summer when it is often a paying job, are the shiniest pennies the university can find in its student body.

If the campus sees itself as intellectual and bookish, the student you meet will likely have those characteristics. If personality and a sunny disposition are held in high esteem, be prepared for one. If leadership preparation is one of the college's goals, your ambassador will likely have a long list of activities and clubs with offices held.

Of course, you want to see how well trained the ambassador is at answering the questions you ask. But most tour guides will be ready and confident, unless the admissions administration is a total shambles, and that would certainly be good to know. Mostly, this is your chance to see, or better, to feel, whether you can be successful here. You will have thirty to forty-five minutes alone (or with your guests) to hear a star student's point of view. No question is off-limits. If the tour guide doesn't know or can't answer, he or she will feel free to let you know. Get a student's opinion about the food, the availability of the faculty, the importance of athletics, the social life, and whatever else matters to you. If your parents are along, see how the guide relates to them. It is important they feel comfortable with your choices as well.

Before you elect to join this ambassador as a student in a little over a year, you will want to talk privately with her and other students, especially those not handpicked by the institution. This can happen on a more intense repeat visit closer to your time of decision. The summer visit is to tell you whether you want to apply. A key question you need to be able to answer right now or soon after leaving campus is whether you can maximize your success at this place.

Remember what matters most in your decision making is whether you will graduate. The goal is to pick a school where you can be happy and successful. Nothing good you observe on a visit about a college justifies your choosing it and then having a miserable experience there.

Myth 22: You can find all kinds of students on any campus.

Reality: Student bodies tend to replicate themselves.

When you're on the tour, consider the tour guide the measure of success walking alongside you here. Do you like him or her? Do you think you would like to live, study, play, and cry with this student and her or his classmates? It is an exaggeration to say that the students will all be alike; surely there will be differences among them. Yet go away for a few years and come back to any campus and the students seem the same. This is not a surprise or a wonder or a mystery: Students are attracted to study by and with those they like, admire, and resemble.

The best way to sort this issue out while you are on the tour is to consider: "Could I see myself leading this tour myself twelve or twenty-four months from now?" This is not purely a thinking thing. You will feel it in your gut. Does it feel right? That intuitive hunch should be listened to loud and clear. It is more important than the charts and color brochures; more vital than the statistics you will be fed. There is no need to make a final determination on the tour or on this day. You are just collecting information and impressions.

Ask a couple of easy questions and let the guide shine with lots of positive vibes. Then ask a tough question or two (try to ask the same one at each campus to get some baseline comparison). You don't have to be interested in the answer really, although if you are, go for it. You are really trying to measure things such as comfort level with tough issues and the openness of conversation on campus. If you can't think of any other questions, ask about alcohol use (they will have heard that one before) or safety (that one gets asked in one form or another all the time) or how people who are different are treated (fill in your own blank, race, gender, sexual orientation, etc.). That might be a new one for the tour guide. Don't push it too hard if she or he gets uncomfortable or flustered. The guide might suggest asking a staff member. But there are some things, maybe many things, better learned from a student. She or he is living here, and you will be too. She or he is here when it is dark and on weekends. Most staff members, and almost all faculty, are not.

Listen closely to what the student guide emphasizes; that will tell you about the things the college values—she or he has been trained to do so. What questions does she or he ask? They might be on behalf of the admissions office, thinking you would rather volunteer answers to a student. They might want to know how serious you are about their school or where else you are applying. Deflect those questions. Keep things to yourself. You are in control and will volunteer what you want to volunteer at the right time for you.

But the questions might be of interest to your student guide, and that's even more important. What do students want to know about each other? Does it matter what kind of car you drive? Or if you have a serious boyfriend or girlfriend, or what you want to study? These are all simple invitations to conversation but also ways to probe how you will fit. Few ambassadors ask these questions with any plan or reason. But what's on her or his mind begins to tell you about the student culture.

Before the tour ends, get the student guide's view on any number of issues that might be of interest to you. You will get many other opinions before you have finished your research, but this is a good beginning and probably tells you what the university wants you to know or think.

Soon after the tour, debrief with any others who accompanied you. Share impressions and see what different perspectives there might be. Most important, see what the others think about how well you would fit in there. Your friends and family know you and how you interact with others. Ultimately, it's your decision not theirs, but the input you receive is valuable as you think through your immediate and long-range decisions.

The tour guide will bring you back to where you started, and now it will be time to sit down with a staff member. This will probably be an admissions counselor or assistant director, and maybe if you are lucky, the one assigned to your high school or region. Get ready; you are about to ask the question you have been waiting all day to get an answer about. (see myth 24 for that question.)

Myth 23: College staff members are checking you out.

Reality: Admissions staff members are a college's sales team and are there to be your advocate for admission.

The relationship you begin to establish with this representative is vital to the next year while you will be applying for admission and financial aid. The counselor will have you meet with lots of other campus people who specialize in academic and business matters. But this representative, or a staff colleague, will be your lifeline to the often complex matters ahead while you are selecting where to attend. Since you will apply to several schools, you will have dialogue with admissions officers at each institution. Often that relationship is central to your decision making. The representatives want you to come to their school. Their pride, and even more their job success, is on the line in the decisions you and other prospective students will be making.

The representative you meet with is seldom the one who makes a decision about whether you will be admitted. That selection usually rests with the admissions director or dean or a committee that this representative meets with to make choices. In fact, your admission rep is really your advocate. He or she will likely help you understand financial aid by introducing you as time goes by to the financial aid staff and talking with you about that process.

Be very open and honest with your representative. There is no point pretending to be someone or something you are not. That façade will only peel away once you are in school anyway. If you are admitted on false pretenses, it only risks that a bad match may have been made. Keep reminding yourself that you are in the driver's seat. This is not the only college on your list. Excited as you may be about it (and it's a good thing if you are), you have other options. It is good to be eager and excited. Colleges love motivated students. But don't get so "up" that you lose perspective or risk big disappointment.

Ask if the representative is a recent graduate of the school. Chances are this will be the case. An excellent student ambassador is often invited to consider spending some time after graduation as an admissions staff member. Once again, the goal is to provide a positive role model of the school's "product." The jobs don't pay much, have long hours with lots of difficult travel, and often lots of disappointments when students being recruited for a year or more choose to go elsewhere. But these jobs are excellent preparation for any sales career and sometimes even lead to lifetime work in college admissions. (Who knows? That could be something for you to think about way down the road.)

You will be invited to sit face-to-face with this new and important friend and mentor. You will probably notice, or at least should, if the representative is well trained, that you are treated differently than in high school meetings. You are being talked to as an equal, as an adult. Welcome to college!

MYTHS ABOUT RETENTION (HOW MANY STUDENTS GRADUATE)

A well-known and respected educational leader was once asked his opinion on extending the time of study for earning a bachelor's degree from the standard four years to five. Given that many undergraduates now do take five years or longer to complete the degree, the case for making the longer time period the norm rather than the exception made sense to some. "Not so," argued the leader in question. He pointed out that half of all high school graduates who start college never finish. Thus, he believed that the fact that colleges now failed to get the job done in four years was hardly a compelling case for requiring still another year of study.

Remember the lesson of myth 2: Very little good comes for anyone from a student's failure to graduate. Myths 24 through 26 should help you make a choice that will result in a success story and lead to your college graduation!

Myth 24: There is nothing profoundly important to learn on the campus visit.

Reality: There is a most important question to ask—the question about graduation rates.

When the time is right on the campus visit, ask the following most important question: "By the way, can you tell me on average how many freshmen return the next year to continue their education here?"

You may not see them, but light bulbs will be going off in the counselor's head. Not many prospective students have the sophistication to raise the issue of what academicians call retention. You are not asking to score points with the counselor (even though you will). You are asking to get an answer—in fact, the most important one you will uncover. Remember our central axiom: You are probing how the campus you are visiting does at educating their students. Your question cuts to the heart of graduating successfully, what in college-speak is called retention.

Eventually, you really will want to know not only what percentage of entering students graduate, but how long it takes them. (The number of years required in practice dramatically impacts the cost of your education and your ability to get started with whatever you will decide to do after you graduate.) For now, that graduation rate question invites too much ambiguity and statistical juggling. So keep it simple: "If x students start in year one, x minus how many return in year two?"

Many of these students will transfer elsewhere and a significant number of them will graduate someplace else. There is nothing necessarily wrong with moving around from one school to another (a surprisingly large number of students do it), but it almost always takes longer to get a degree that way. Your goal should be to make the right decision the first time as to where you can be successful, knowing that sometimes circumstances can change and you can always do something else later. So the answer the counselor gives provides you with important information. We'll examine these answers in myth 25.

> **Myth 25:** Students withdraw from college throughout their undergraduate careers.
>
> **Reality:** The overwhelming majority of students who leave without a degree do so before the start of their second year.

When you ask a counselor about their school's retention rate, you are bound to get one of four response. Here is a way to gauge the four basic responses:

Response One: "Oh I am glad you asked, we do very well at that here. It's one of real strengths. Usually upward of 80 percent of our students return for their sophomore year."

This is usually the preferred response (although it does need a follow-up). The higher the number, the better. Once it is in the 80 percent+ range, things are going well on that campus.

Do ask a follow-up question, because the success may be in the students being recruited rather than any proactive college effort. Ask the following question: "Do you know why you are having that success?" Since the school is doing well bringing its students back, they probably understand why.

Hopefully, it is the result of some strategic decisions, but it may be that they only recruit top students who almost always persist at a high rate.

Perhaps they attract a very homogeneous student body, especially if the school has a very specific church relationship and/or is in a remote, rural location. The former president of one such school used to tell first-time guests, "Now that you have found us, you know why 95 percent of our freshmen return . . . once you get here, you can't leave." Although that self-deprecating humor is amusing, there is a grain of truth. Even more importantly, that particular college recruited many, many students from the same denomination and part of the country. If you are a part of the group that represents the majority of the student body, and you might be if you choose to visit after doing your prospecting, the dynamic producing persistence might work for you as well. But if on your visit you feel like an outsider or want to be at a place with lots of different kinds of students, maybe a warning bell has sounded.

Response Two: "What a good question. You know we really work at that and have made some dramatic recent strides, but I have to be honest and tell you that about a third or sometimes more of our first-year students don't return for the second year."

This is a problem area, but not absolutely fatal. Give the school points for honesty and even more for being aware there is a problem and for consciously trying to work at it. In fact, a case can be made that a school with lower numbers but with an awareness and a desire to get better might be more interested in your success than one that has high retention but has been on automatic pilot about the issue. They might not be as attentive to your issues once you enroll. Regardless, there is obviously something to be alarmed about here. One out of three or worse is a risky number for you.

The follow-up question here is "Why has the rate been so low?" Do they enroll a number of nontraditional learners (e.g., part-time, older, commuters)? Do they take some calculated chances on students who might not be accepted elsewhere? Is there substantial diversity in the student body? Do they serve areas where the academic preparation of students may not be consistently thorough? Any of these factors might reduce retention rates but perhaps create a campus environment that might be more conducive to learning for a particular student.

Response Three: "You know, I am a little embarrassed but I am not sure of that number. I do know the dean of students keeps close tabs on that, and if I can't reach that office while you are here, I will email you an answer in the next couple of days."

This is a nonresponse you can live with for a little while. If the school cares enough, many people will have your answer and the admissions team especially should be trained on what to say. Again, give the school a few points here for honesty, and maybe the follow-up will be fine. It is good to learn that someone important on campus cares about retention. If a response is delayed or if it is unsatisfactory, you might need to cross this school off your list.

Response Four: "Wow, that's a new one. Honestly, I don't think we track that kind of information. Why do you ask?"

This is the answer you absolutely don't want to hear because it suggests that very little proactive attention is paid by the school to student success. You are visiting more schools than you should apply to anyway, so it's good to find an easy one to cut. It is doubtful, however, you will get this response very much anymore. An enormous amount of attention in higher education circles has focused on retention, or attrition as it is called when looking at the problem, not the goal.

Myth 26: It pays to go to college.

Reality: College only pays off for those who get out the right way, with a degree.

Let's stop and think about the importance of the question you asked in myth 24 and the answers you received in myth 25. It costs a tremendous amount of time, effort, and money to recruit students. As with any business, this expense is only justified if the student (customer) keeps returning. Colleges used to (but can no longer afford to) keep recruiting large class after large class, knowing that many of their students wouldn't stick around. Why go to school where you can't be reasonably satisfied that the institution wants you to be successful and knows how to help make that happen?

Remember that it is never better to fail to graduate from Elite College, no matter its fancy reputation, than it is to graduate from Not-So-Elite College. College graduates earn twice as much an average in their lifetime than noncollege graduates. The investment made, if you fail to complete a degree, just isn't worth it. For-profit businesses, who study customer persistence much more closely than higher education does, know that if someone doesn't buy from them again that "the product isn't good enough." They don't act as if the customer has let them down or is being disloyal. Rather they do their research and retool to improve what they are selling.

Higher education blames the student for failing to achieve the desired goal. Ask students whether they would have enrolled if the college didn't offer degrees. The question, in itself, is so absurd—of course, they wouldn't. Yet many, many students will leave without having accomplished what they came after.

There is always a risk of not succeeding and, of course, students need to do their part by taking their college careers seriously. But with so many choices out there for places to study, why not pay attention to schools that understand they have a responsibility also to students to do everything they can to make the "product" better?

Such emphasis on retention is good business practice for a college. It makes sense to work to bring students back semester after semester. Airlines reward frequent flyers. Colleges should equally value their repeat customers. Not only do students who persist to graduation provide ongoing revenue, they also deliver powerful testimonials to future students about the value and benefit of the school they are attending.

MYTHS ABOUT THE APPLICATION PROCESS

Admissions directors have very different approaches to selectivity. Two legendary and highly successful, long-time directors were diametrically opposite. One always worried about numbers and tried to admit almost everyone. His faculty admissions committee had to watch doggedly to make sure he didn't slip unqualified candidates into the entering class. The other wanted to build appeal by making it almost impossible to be admitted. His committee had to scratch and claw to get anyone accepted.

Oddly and interestingly, both schools succeeded beyond anyone's wildest expectations. Maybe it didn't matter which approach was applied, or maybe the faculty committees brought each place toward their optimum admissions strategy.

Having a short list of colleges in your back pocket as late August rolls around will feel good. A year from now you will drive onto your campus, the place you will graduate from, knowing you have made the right decision. It is vital to figure out where to apply. If a school gets cut at this stage, you will likely never think about it again. Let's take a good bit of time in myths 27 through 39 so you know where to apply and how to get those applications done comfortably before December.

Myth 27: Colleges can get along without you.

Reality: You are the reason why the school exists, and without you (and your peers) it would be closed.

Pay particular attention to the way campuses treat you after your visit. You have blown your cover now. They know you are a hot prospect, and chances are they will follow up eagerly. Certainly, anything you asked to have sent should arrive quickly and accurately. A school will be telling you a great deal about how efficient they are and how interested in you they seem by their follow-up. Expect a letter from a high-ranking official, maybe even the president. (Some schools might have tried to get you a quick introduction with the president or another senior official on your visit. If not, see if you can make that happen if or when you return.) Although the president might not have personally signed your letter, it is still a nice touch suggesting accessibility and a priority to students.

Colleges usually plan for a fairly specific number of new students. To get that number, and to see how they are progressing toward that target goal, they track just about everything: prospect contacts, visits, and especially, applications. They compare all these numbers to previous years to see how they are doing.

The number of applications received is the most accurate and important predictor of the size of an entering class that colleges track. They talk about their conversion rate, which is the percentage of new students who will enroll from all the applications received. This rate doesn't vary much from year to year or even school to school. Most students actually apply to two to four schools. So it follows that conversion rates are usually 30 percent to 40 percent; that is, three or four enrolled students for every ten applicants.

Colleges know they will not convert the majority of their applicants. It's sort of like success for a baseball hitter: 3 hits in 10 at bats means a .300 batting average, which for ballplayers and colleges is quite good. Yet, for both enterprises, there is little margin for error or greatness: 3.5 for 10 is all-star material; 4 in 10 almost never happens; and yet 2 for 10 won't keep a player or a college in business long.

One useful technique you can use might be sort of a secret "straw ballot" of your own. A few days after your last campus visit of the summer, sit down and write on a sheet of paper the top five schools you would apply to if you had to make that decision right then. Tuck that paper away someplace safe and check and revise it every few weeks throughout the fall. This is a handy way to keep score for yourself as to where you are leaning to apply.

Myth 28: Colleges assume you will apply and will attend if admitted.

Reality: Colleges know that competition for you will be costly, and they may not win.

Don't be surprised if the colleges that you visited go for a preemptive financial strike to get you to say you are coming their way. They know you are looking at several other campuses, so they may try to turn your head by offering something attractive early. They won't always do so, and don't be too depressed if it doesn't happen. Colleges won't advertise that they make early aid awards because they want you to be so surprised and flattered if it happens that you will be really tempted to say yes.

By now they are armed with your test scores, high school performance, and some sophisticated information from your interview about your financial circumstances. You probably sent or gave them your scores and transcript (that's a smart thing to do). Admissions folks are trained to ask good questions and keep their eyes open. The school now knows what you may intend to study, whether you have siblings in college, what your parents do for a living, what kind of neighborhood you live in, and probably what you are driving. Armed with that intelligence, they can make remarkably accurate guesses of what kind of financial aid you will be offered after the long, complicated process to determine aid that lies ahead.

If you are a student they want, why shouldn't they go ahead and let you know that once you apply they will guarantee you a certain level of financial award? The promise will be that this early aid award, based on merit and predicted need, will be the least they will do, but they might do more when you fill out the required financial forms later. Rest assured they are not hurting themselves.

By this point in the process, colleges have developed fairly detailed aid budgets. They know about how much they will take from their tuition revenue and, like Robin Hood, will divide that amount up among their prospective students to make the education they offer affordable and to get the students they really want. If by offering you a little less early on than what they figure they may have to spend ultimately to get you to enroll, they know they will win by saving a few dollars to be used for other students. They also hope you will feel you win because you have an early secure offer and might be ready to shorten up the whole shopping process by accepting it and making your college choice earlier than you expected.

Of course, since schools all know the rules of engagement used now in the college search process, you might actually receive more than one school's early indication of a financial aid award. If so, that weakens the bargaining position of the colleges making the offer because students figure out that they are witnessing a marketing technique more than a unique offer of special circumstances.

Myth 29: An early indication of enthusiasm on the school's part is a very positive, unusual sign.

Reality: A preliminary financial aid award offer underestimates what you will receive in calculations based on ability and need.

Colleges will tell you in small print that an early financial aid award is contingent on admission, high school graduation, no serious decline in your senior-year academic performance, and the documentation of any self-reported information. But you have an offer, and it will be darn tempting. DO NOT UNDER ANY CIRCUMSTANCES ACCEPT IT!

You are in control of this process, and they are trying to cut your decision making short. Even if they say they won't, colleges will make you that offer, and usually more, months later at the regular point in the process. You have time. Play the process out. You have a lot more to learn before you can be sure where you will be successful. The key question is not getting in but finding out where you can be successful. Don't lose courage. Trust yourself. You still need to and can figure out where you will decide to go to earn your degree.

Parents, friends, and advisors may urge and even try to berate you into taking the first offer you get. It would gain you lots of time in the months ahead if you just ended the process now. That motivation is exactly what colleges making early offers are hoping you will be thinking. It would be so tempting to let grandma, the hometown paper, and the world know where you are going to college. It would be so sweet to be all wrapped up and set before the rest of your friends have made their decisions.

But there is so much more to learn before making your choice. If you doubt yourself, the safety net of an offer in hand is very seductive. Remember the lesson from myth 1: It is only to the college's advantage to cause you to retain the notion that they are in control of the process. Everything you are learning here is to strengthen your resolve that you are in control.

Colleges don't have to let you in, so it seems risky to remain selective yourself. Please have the confidence to remain selective. Colleges will keep on coming back to you even if you play it a little cool with them. Sixty to seventy percent or more of their applicants will reject them. The longer you wait, within reason, the more they are likely to sweeten the pot to attract you as a new student. Chances are good that their offer to you will remain on the table all the way through to the late spring, when most students make their final college selection.

So write a very nice letter thanking them for making the early offer. Tell them (unless it isn't so) that you remain very interested but that you are sure they would want you to take your time so that when you decide you will be absolutely certain. Encourage your representative to stay in close touch with you. Request whatever you feel might be helpful in the way of more information. And tell them to hold onto that financial aid offer, you might well be back to collect it!

Myth 30: Colleges don't care much about where else you are looking.

Reality: Schools want to pry from you information about your other "short-list" places.

Colleges aren't going to tell you everything about their side of the recruitment process. The more complex it seems to you, the scarier it can become. So why should you be expected to tell them everything about your search? Keep the scales of power here as balanced as you can.

Besides, colleges probably can make good guesses about where else you are looking. Colleges study closely what schools students cross-apply to against them. Admissions is a remarkably competitive business. They want to know where else you are looking so they can study the competitive advantages and disadvantages of those other schools against their programs and facilities. That way, they can calculate a recruitment strategy to their advantage, not yours.

If they are the only small school you are looking at, they can deduce that the hustle and bustle of a big school is probably tempting you. So they will work hard to show you the advantages of a smaller place and try to convince you that there is plenty to do. If they have a fraternity/sorority system and your other schools don't, they will be apt to get current Greek students with you to talk about the advantages and downplay the shortcomings of Greek life on campus.

Colleges have experience and expertise on their side. They have gone through this process time after time. For you it is a new and once-in-a-lifetime opportunity. Giving schools too much information gives them an advantage to fast-talk you. Take your time to make a decision at your own pace. Keep your own counsel. Share what you want with who you want when you want to do so.

Schools know how other schools recruit for a student of your ability. They know how aggressive the competition will be and how much financial aid might be dangled at various phases of the process. Why give them this much information? Remain a bit mysterious. It usually results in you seeming more attractive.

Myth 31: Colleges will get all the applications they need.

Reality: Colleges will do whatever they can to get you to apply.

The ultimate goal for a college's admissions effort is to recruit a freshman class of the size and quality the school believes is optimal for its program, structure, and budget. By the end of the process, this effort means individually working with as many students as possible to convince them to enroll. Earlier in the process, however, colleges know that to have the result they want at the end, they must generate a sufficient number of qualified applicants. So, the colleges you are looking at know that they need to be on that final short list of schools you will apply to for admission.

Schools will, or should, work very hard to turn you into an applicant. If you sense that they are half-hearted or disorganized, it is a legitimate reason to make that tough decision to cut them from your final grouping. They will have no problem cutting you if they think you don't fit. Fair is fair!

Look for incentives to get you to apply. Many schools, in hopes of getting applications early, or at all, will offer substantial rewards for meeting certain deadlines, such as

- Application fee waivers
- Bookstore vouchers
- Clothing and other paraphernalia
- Free transportation to return for another visit
- Campus entertainment tickets

• The promise of eligibility for some premier campus housing or parking

If there is something you might want but don't see offered, don't hesitate to ask. Colleges will never want you more than they do at this stage of the process. They know you are cutting a number of the schools you have visited and been interested in before.

It doesn't make sense to file too many applications. If you cut a school before applying, chances are they will never have another shot at recruiting you. Their applicant pool will be the group they work exclusively with in the months ahead. Admission representatives usually have goals of how many applications they must generate from their areas of responsibility. Even if a school may not have a policy to provide something extra to help you once you apply, chances are your rep will bend over backward to get that application on file. Electronic filing is now commonplace and can be easy and fun. Having you in among the applicants is much desired. You may well be surprised at how hard your schools work to get you there.

One caveat; if you are likely planning to be an athlete competing in intercollegiate athletics: The National Collegiate Athletic Association (NCAA) has very strict rules about what may and may not be done to recruit prospective athletes. Compliance with these regulations is closely enforced and monitored. So athletes beware, there will likely be few goodies in your baskets. If there are, be even more careful. The few schools that play fast and loose with these rules are almost always headed for a day of reckoning that will likely impact all their current and future student athletes for a long time.

Myth 32: Some students only apply to small colleges.

Reality: Almost everyone applies to a "flagship" state university.

Some schools have so much household name recognition that they generate many, many applications without much effort. The big state universities have legions of alumni, all kinds of television time for their well-known sports teams, and thousands of students. They need very large entering classes and will get them. Most students seriously consider at least one such flagship place and usually apply there. Sometimes students are leaving their options open and want to have admission to such a well-known institution in their back pocket for financial or ego reasons.

State universities are usually less expensive for in-state students than other private or far-away options. Or perhaps students want to be able to brag that they were admitted to the "U"—even if they have no intention of going there (especially if a family member is an alumnus of the school). Or, if prospecting and visiting haven't been done well, the highly visible state university might be the only option known. Finally, it probably matters that an application to a place everyone has heard of is much easier to explain. In fact, such a decision probably requires no explanation or justification to friends, counselors, and parents.

Such premier state schools have remarkably successful graduate and professional programs. They almost always train most of the state's doctors, dentists, and attorneys. Their alumni are fiercely loyal and visible. Although they usually have the most dollars for advertising and media relations, they need the least since everyone in the state, even at a very early age, can identify their locations, colors, mascots, and fight songs. Everything about these places is well known and highly publicized. These large schools have active social and cultural lives with popular speakers and many, many diverse activities and organizations to appeal to every possible personal taste or interest.

On the other hand, large campuses can be impersonal. It might be difficult for students to get much personal attention or opportunity. Problems can sometimes go unnoticed. Sadly, some students fall prey to serious issues with alcohol, although that deep social problem is not reserved to just one kind of campus or age group.

In most states, there is a second and even sometimes third tier of public universities, many of them founded years and years ago as teacher training colleges, although today they are somewhat more comprehensive. These schools may be smaller and a bit more attentive to undergraduates than the flagship, research universities. Often they are less selective and can take chances on students who may not have had spotless academic high school records. But these schools also can have the anonymity and social problems of the major state university without the benefit of the world-class intellectual resources found at the most highly regarded public university in the state.

Roughly 75 percent of American undergraduate degrees are awarded at large, public state university campuses. The mission of these institutions to inexpensively educate all who qualify is remarkable and unique and represents the most far-reaching accomplishment of any higher education system in the world, past or present. As big as these schools are, there is always a risk that some students may fall through the cracks and not receive the kind of personal attention they deserve. However, that doesn't and shouldn't happen too often. Colleges spend a great deal of money and effort to make sure their systems work. If you feel something is lacking in their approach to you, by all means inquire of their admissions office. Great educations are available in America's great universities. You might have to work a little harder to access all they have available, but it is usually worth the effort.

Myth 33: Great faculty will be available to undergraduate students.

Reality: What faculty contact you will have depends mostly on the size of the school.

Applying to the biggest, best-known school on your list is an easy decision. This university will likely enroll more than twenty thousand undergraduates like you. In addition, it is probably wise to pick one of the most attractive smaller schools you have visited as you work to complete your choices to which you will apply. These smaller places will likely be private and often church-related with student bodies of fewer that 2,500 students. Then, for number three, you might pick a mid-sized school of say five thousand to ten thousand students. In this category, you will have many options of both public and private schools. This way you are keeping your options open. You will have chosen your most viable option from each category determined essentially by the size of the school.

How much contact with your teachers (in college they are called faculty) you will have is an important variable to stay informed about. Of course, not every student learns the same way nor expects the same degree of personal attention. Many students thrive on being well known and having a mentor-like relationship with one or more faculty. Others are quite comfortable being less well known.

Of course, even in the largest schools, students tend to develop some close ties with professors they work more closely with in the later, more advanced stages of their education, as juniors and seniors, for example. These contacts are very important in helping garner the letters of reference many students need for admission to graduate and professional schools or in job applications.

By and large, the big universities have research agendas for their faculty, who must help get and maintain external funding for programs and stay involved actively in their professions and fields, especially through contact with colleagues and advanced graduate students, not undergraduates. The job descriptions for faculty at smaller schools tend to focus more on working with undergraduate students, although to be sure, professors at these places have much heavier teaching loads. They may usually be teaching three or four different classes in each semester, where at larger schools the teaching load might be one or two preparations each term.

There is a vigorous debate about the role of graduate-student teaching assistants in undergraduate instruction. Critics complain that large universities depend too much on graduate students to teach undergrads. The argument is made that the great professors are on campus but not visible in the undergraduate experience or classroom. Small schools take pride in saying that all students are taught by faculty. Yet, those faculty may be far

removed from the newest breakthroughs in their
fields, and some wonder if a recently educated
teaching assistant might not be more able to share
those findings with students in a more active
research university setting. There are no absolutes in
the debates about teaching and research. Probably
your best route is to talk seriously with your former
high school classmates who are now in their first
college years, those students whose opinions and
experience you respect. Ask them what they think of
graduate assistants as teachers. Find out how much
contact they can have with faculty stars. Use their
perspectives to help sharpen your own.

Myth 34: What you want to study should
determine where you apply.

Reality: You can major in almost anything,
almost anywhere.

More fuss is made about what you are going to study,
the so-called major, than is really useful or necessary. Schools work very hard to establish a niche,
something for which they are well known. But the

curriculum (what you will study) is pretty much the same everywhere, and the faculty at most schools have similar training and backgrounds. Even the professions (medicine, nursing, and engineering) either require advanced study for which there is no specific preparation or can be prepared for at schools that do not specialize in these fields exclusively.

Of course, there are exceptions. You would probably want to study oceanography or marine biology at a school that's close to water. But art history can be learned far away from museums, and Hispanic culture can be studied on the Canadian border. Perhaps a case can be made for faculty expertise in certain fields, but again remember that the well-known faculty stars are known for their publications primarily and won't have much exposure to undergraduates.

For the past generation, most faculty fields have been oversupplied. Although that will be changing as baby boomer–generation faculty retire in large numbers, it is still generally the case that smaller, more remote colleges have benefited from this oversupply by hiring fine faculty from excellent graduate programs. Students have been the beneficiaries of the wider distribution of faculty talent and expertise. Many years ago, it may have been the case that only a handful of colleges provided high-quality instruction in some fields. Now a student can get an excellent education and preparation for career, professional school, or graduate program just about anywhere.

Colleges compete so hard to make their programs distinctive, yet it is still very difficult for them to demonstrate uniqueness given the hundreds, indeed thousands, of peer, competing institutions. What separates one campus from another may have far more to do with the quality of experience and opportunity outside the classroom. It is important to validate the academic quality of the schools you wish to apply to and possibly attend. However, the real distinction may have less to do with what is taught than with how instruction is delivered and the support system that exists to make sure you are successful.

Many successful alumni point out that what really made a difference in defining their future success happened outside the classroom, perhaps in on-the-job internship experiences or even in extracurricular activities. Leadership, problem solving, ethics, critical thinking, and decision making are all subjects of formal academic study. Yet most graduates, ten or twenty years down the road, seem to believe the application of theory in practice provided the teachable moments that served them well in their careers and lives. Or, put another way, it has been noted that students come to a campus to learn how to make a living, but while there, they do also learn how to make a life.

Myth 35: You had better know what you want to major in when you apply.

Reality: "Undecided" is the largest major in the freshman class.

A major is something almost all colleges require. Colleges want to see that you can add layer upon layer of knowledge and understanding in a particular field. You will spend roughly one-third of your academic time studying history or chemistry or nursing.

Some majors are professional. In these majors, after passing a licensure test, you graduate ready for the first steps in your career. Examples of these majors are nursing, teaching, engineering, or accounting, where you are a professional upon graduation.

Other majors are preprofessional. They lead you to graduate or professional school but not to the profession itself. Usually, many roads lead to professional school, so most campuses have programs that are packaged as pre-med, or pre-law, but really the actual campus major is fairly wide open. Most students who go to medical school major in biology or chemistry, but they don't have to do so. Law school candidates often major in political science, English, history, or philosophy, but some concentrate in art or theatre or some other specialty.

The last cluster of majors is not at all career specific. Although it is hard to get parents to value a concentration in art history or literature, many of the nation's leaders have this kind of liberal arts major on their college transcripts. Parents need to relax. No one ever hired a major or a transcript. People hire people with talents and attributes that appear to be well suited for the tasks at hand. A few months out of school, no one remembers or cares what you majored in at school. Rather they want to know what you are doing and how well you are prepared to do it.

Besides the major, the bulk of college academic work is either study in required general education, as defined by the faculty, or in elective classes (the real fun stuff). When else in your life will you be able to read Shakespeare or study film aesthetics or learn music theory and get credit for it?

Nationally, 20 percent of all students don't know what they want to major in when they get to college. Schools don't really know what to do with these students. They don't fit neatly into structured programs. They take up more advisor time and, not surprisingly, often graduate at rates lower than the student body in general.

Colleges define students without a major as a problem and blame it on the students themselves. The very term "undecided" suggests a socially embarrassing condition. Students have names and hometowns. They are supposed to have majors.

Don't be afraid to say you are undecided if you are. In fact, one tactic to try would be to say so even if you are not to see how well a college responds to your needs, helps you define your goals, and even has its programs compete to show you their advantages. Helping you find your major, your intellectual passion, your story to tell is one of a college's great opportunities. Finding the place that will work with you to do that may be the ultimate key to the college choice process!

Myth 36: Few people change their major.

Reality: A majority of students are actually undecided and change their majors.

Half of all students who list a major on an application will change that major before graduating. Many change several times, often between the time they apply and when they actually begin school.

Colleges consider such students as problems. Too often, colleges want eighteen-year-olds to behave like career professionals. Admissions committees turn down students who seem to be wandering from field to field. Schools try to match their faculty, classroom, and learning resources with student demand. Change makes them skittish because they worry if they are deployed correctly to serve their students. Students are frequently expected to fit themselves into tidy little boxes that colleges have organized into departments and divisions.

One thing to look for is whether colleges are willing to take the risk on you defining your own special major or cluster of major and minor programs. Why not? One professor sensed the problem of colleges trying to make students line up in accord with the programs they offered and wondered if anyone had ever asked the learners, "What do you want to know?"

Somehow students are supposed to be finished products even before they have started college. If that's the case, why do they need to go? Just award them their degrees before they start if they are expected to be so proficient. Everyone loves the well-organized, highly motivated student. Why not? Who wouldn't want to teach this wonderful student? But maybe learning also occurs when there has been change or disappointment to manage. Everyone hits that wall at some point. There is no better place than a great college environment to learn to experiment with change. Wouldn't it be nice to have an advisor in life who could sign petitions to get us out of jams?

In fact, colleges are more tolerant of career change within the ranks of seasoned professionals (they even encourage it with a variety of reentry programs) than they are when a freshman changes his or her mind about a major between the time they apply and when they enroll. College faculty and administrators will make fun (behind their backs and sometimes to their face) of students who said they were biology/pre-med but now want to choose social work because of a summer internship experience. Those same college employees, whose salaries are being paid by students, might be exploring their own career counseling because of job burn-out, but don't see the inconsistency.

The moral of this tale is to be as honest and open as you can be in your application. You want to know that the school understands it exists to serve your needs. How you are treated throughout this process will really help make your final decision about where to study, and that ought to be at a place that is most likely going to help you be successful, whatever issues or inconveniences to them you might be bringing along.

Remember, the college experience and goal should be ultimately about your success. It is OK, maybe even desirable, to try out different strategies as a student. The right college for you can help rather than hinder your process of self-discovery.

Myth 37: The application essay will make or break your chances.

Reality: Your application, even your essay, may not be read all that closely.

You should of course do the best job you can on the applications you submit, whether online or by mail. It makes sense to put your best foot forward in all you do, and a serious mistake in the application could hurt your chances. But don't make an essay requirement out to be more than it is—just another hurdle and piece of a complex process.

Colleges use essays to get some less-than-serious candidates to give up without having to be rejected. Admissions offices have delicate relationships with high school counselors, and if too many counselors' candidates are rejected that doesn't bode well for getting future applications from that school. For colleges this is a long-term, continuous process. For you it just happens once.

No matter the debate about entrance test validity referenced in myth 4, many schools still find it easier and more convenient to base their decision about you on data—class rank, test scores—without much attention to applications or letters of reference. If your numbers are clearly good enough for the school, you will probably be admitted. If they are not, you will likely be rejected. The essay matters on the margin or borderline. Most of these cases go to a committee made up of faculty. They are more likely to read the essay, but even there they deal with many applicants in a meeting of perhaps an hour once a week.

Impressions matter. In this day of grammar and spell checkers there is no excuse for sloppy work. A few genuinely creative approaches to the essay may catch someone's attention, but reactions to originality might vary greatly. Sadly, it is probably best for your essay to go unnoticed rather than making risky waves.

Students still fret over every nuance of the application and essay. Think about it. How do colleges even know it is your work? How many hundreds of thousands of essays have been written by parents? In this day of Internet accessibility, how hard is it to get an essay from an online source? Some schools have abandoned requiring an essay for these reasons. Even if they do require essays, schools don't possibly have the time and people to read them all carefully. Requiring an essay is one of the ways colleges send subtle messages to their students and faculty. Somehow its inclusion is supposed to signal a seriousness of academic purpose. There is often more form than substance to the requirement.

One exception to the rule about essays not mattering may be if you are a top applicant and might be competing for a very handsome scholarship.

Many schools hold competitions for these awards. In choosing who to invite, and especially who might win, the essay is probably perused more seriously. Even there, however, the face-to-face interview is more important. And don't forget that schools will be using these competitions to attract an array of the kind of students they want, so they will balance the winners by gender, home area, major, and whatever other variables matter to them.

Do a careful, comprehensive job with the applications. Do it for yourself. That's what matters most anyway. Feel good about your choices and your work. You have done what you need to do very thoroughly. The application is just the last step of the first part of the process of being a successful college graduate.

Myth 38: Colleges need to charge an application fee.

Reality: The application fee is not about the money.

Colleges require a nonrefundable application fee, sometimes a hefty one, mostly because they always have done so and most everyone still does. They want to know you are serious enough about them to go to the trouble of applying, and they want you to think that if it so expensive just to apply, the college must be of a high quality. They also don't want you applying to many places since that likely will increase how hard they will have to work to compete. Everything about their process is thought out for its effect. Little is left to chance. They have not built the application structure to work to your advantage but to theirs.

The application fee sends a strong message that less-than-serious students should not apply (since they won't want to spend the money to do so). Think about it. Few other businesses would put a nuisance fee in the way of their potential customers.

Some schools have abandoned the application fee arguing that the junk applications that might be encouraged are a small price to pay for the accessibility they are providing to students and the numbers of applications generated. They want a chance to work to recruit you, so they want your application. Fees discourage some applications.

Perhaps a final decision on your part about where to apply might be made on the basis of the application fee policies of your favorite schools. Some schools might waive fees for online applications or if you have visited campus. These schools are using the fee, or actually the fee waiver, as an enticement. They have a fee in place so they can look for reasons to make you feel good when they waive it.

Take advantage of such policies and choose to apply to schools that make your interest a central factor in their decision making. That's a very good indicator that they will continue to help as you enroll and progress toward graduation. Have they built a process that benefits you? Schools that are genuinely student focused are just as intentional about their admissions strategies as are those that put their institution's interest above the students'. In fact, you wouldn't really want to be at a college that was sloppy with the way it handled things. You want to be able to depend on their effective management.

But running a truly student-centered operation is still the exception, not the rule. On too many campuses, students are seen as problems and not as opportunities. You are not an interruption, although you will likely often be made to feel that way. Colleges wouldn't exist without you. Higher education has been slow to recognize that it is a service industry. Some colleges have caught on to this reality. Those are the ones you are trying to identify, and where you will be best served to apply.

Myth 39: Accepting a school's early offer of admission relieves a great deal of student stress.

Reality: The "early decision" option is totally to the school's advantage.

As part of the application, some schools will ask if you want to be considered as an "early decision" applicant. This means that your admission decision is made earlier, on a much faster track than is typical. These are schools that generally let students know if they are accepted on April 1 and expect a decision from the student by May 1. Many other schools are on a rolling admission basis and will let you know if you are accepted within a few weeks of receiving your application.

The April 1/May 1 schools tend to be more exclusive or selective in their decision making. They want to, and can get away with, holding all the cards because students are willing to play the game. Keeping your decision-making hostage to their timelines takes away much chance for you to exercise control over your admission process. They can wait all year to make their minds up, but they want you to decide with the clock ticking. Is this high-pressure way how they will treat your education and progress toward graduation once you are a student?

To further reduce your opportunity to make an informed choice, the April 1/May 1 schools want to know that if they admit you by December 1, you will decide to attend them and prematurely end your college search. They know that such early-decision reasoning is tempting to consider, especially if you see yourself on the borderline for admission. The notion is that maybe the school will admit you if you apply for early decision but might not admit you if you wait for April 1 to go head-to-head with all their other applicants. In reality, early decision gives colleges a better feel for how to balance the rest of their decisions. Once they know the gender, ethnic, and quality mix of this first section of their next entering class, they can reprioritize remaining applicants to make sure they mix up the class as they want to structure it.

Recently, some very selective colleges have bent to pressure and have abandoned the option. Minority students, in particular, have felt pressured to grab spots via early decision and limited their search options. Forcing the beginning abandonment of a practice like early decision is a positive sign that perhaps colleges are beginning to respond positively to consumer pressure from students and their advocates.

Have more faith in yourself and in your decision making rather than call off your search by accepting an early-decision offer. The school wants you to take yourself out of the process you have set in motion. They are not doing you a favor as a student. Rather, the college is filling some strategically designed quota or percentage of students it wants locked in by December 1. Once you accept their offer, they don't have to court you anymore. Energy and money can be spent on others. Make them worry about you. They will probably still want you April 1. If they don't, others will. Take the risk.

Myths about Financial Aid

The following is a sad but true story:

A woman, recently widowed, pulled into a car dealership. She was driving an expensive European-made vehicle that her late husband had purchased on an impulse just before his unexpected death. She was desperate to trade it in so she could buy a new American sedan just like she had always driven, and the dealership was eager to comply. The woman, delighted at the prospect of having her kind of car back, and unfamiliar with the ways of the car lot, wrote a check for the sticker price minus a very modest trade-in on her highly desirable import. She could have saved a large sum of money by negotiating a better deal on the price of the car she was buying and the amount being offered for her trade-in. As the widow drove out blissfully untutored in the ways of dealing for cars, the sales force couldn't believe their good fortune.

The story still makes the rounds of that dealership years later. No one who hears it can believe the widow's innocence in the ways of the marketplace. Yet those same people have been paying the tuition "sticker price" for their kids' college education every year without thinking that they have any other choice. There is much valuable information to be learned in becoming an informed consumer of higher education. Myths 40 through 52 will teach you the basics you need to know.

Myth 40: Colleges have a well-thought-out financial assistance vision and strategy.

Reality: Colleges have been playing a dangerous high-tuition/high-aid game for several decades without much thought to its long-term sustainability.

It is becoming increasingly difficult for American families to earn enough, save enough, and invest enough to keep pace with the soaring cost of college educations. There is a real possibility that at some point, the ordinary American family might throw in the towel and say that a college education just isn't worth it.

College costs have steadily spiraled out of control for several decades. Not a year has gone by where college tuition increases have not exceeded the inflation rate often by several percentage points. Clever administrators have convinced themselves and others that the general inflation rate shouldn't apply to higher education because of the technology and labor intensity of their enterprise. But even the so-called higher education inflation rate, pegged at 2 percent above the quoted national rate, has been regularly exceeded. Yet schools basically charge what they think the market, with great difficulty, can bear.

Colleges think their price increases don't really matter because they have also witnessed and directed a huge increase in financial aid. This has allegedly been done to match the tuition increases. (Even if that were true, it would be silly, since if both tuition and aid increase at the same rate, no new net income would result.) But obviously, aid increases, however dramatic, have not kept pace with rising tuition costs, and students are paying more. Even more dangerously, much of the student-aid awards, to keep up with rising costs, have been built on loans or borrowed money. At some point, these must usually be repaid. Default rates and the debt loads of students are factors that need to be closely monitored.

As complex and boring as it might be, you will need to discover how schools you are thinking about attending address these cost and aid issues. Do they work to make it understandable to you where the money comes from and goes? Is there student input on at least some aspects of financial decisions? Are price increase justifications explained? If tuition goes up well beyond the inflation rate, is it clear how your education will benefit as a result?

You do need to plan how to make your college choice affordable. There are very specific actions you can take throughout the process to do so. Before providing instructions, it is important to understand the financial environment in which colleges operate.

Myth 41: Colleges tuition costs are determined by what schools need to spend.

Reality: How much a college charges has more to do with positioning the institution in the marketplace.

We live in a consumer culture where value and price have become synonymous. A $40,000 car is assumed to be twice as good a $20,000 car. A $40,000 college must then be twice as good as a $20,000 college, right?

The Federal Trade Commission prohibits colleges from sharing pricing decisions in advance of their being made. But even so, schools put other schools' tuition decisions under the microscope once they become public information (or are leaked from internal communications or other sources). Every school keeps a list of how their tuition stacks up against others. Administrators and trustees study where their tuition ranks vis-à-vis their competition. Decisions about what to charge are frequently based on a strategy to move up the list to appear to be a higher-quality school.

Colleges have had so little interest or success in finding good outcome measures of what students really learn that they are forced to depend upon price (or entrance exams or magazine polls) to determine quality. With no standard gauge of productivity, and with no profit or bottom line to measure, financial benchmarks take on an all-too-important role in evaluating institutional health.

Every subgroup of employees, especially faculty, closely monitors economic factors. Salaries of faculty by rank are collected nationally and made available at least once a year. Tremendous pressure is brought by faculty associations, and in some states, unions, to keep pace or exceed what colleagues at peer institutions are being paid. Librarians study what percentage of college budgets is spent on learning resources. Information officers do the same for computer technology and services. No one is ever satisfied. More resources are always the request.

Colleges have few sources of revenue. Gifts, grants, and auxiliary enterprises (bookstore, food service, etc.), while vital, pale in comparison to the revenue generated by student enrollments. Thus colleges go back to the well of tuition dollars time and again to address their financial situation and their reputation.

These big-picture decisions about budgets and competition are played out at a level far removed from the needs of individual students, and so it must be. Yet college administrators don't need to lose sight of the individuals being impacted by their decisions. It is important to remember that students do at some point experience the consequences. You may well want to investigate whether the schools you are exploring do pay this kind of attention to your situation. Is the president or the chief financial officer available to meet with groups of students to disclose financial information? Discovering that these kinds of meetings occur on a campus, and they do at some, would be a pretty obvious message that it is the sort of school where your learning might well flourish.

Myth 42: Colleges are under pressure to hold costs down.

Reality: Schools are charging far more than they need to in order to achieve some sort of marketing strategy.

A few schools have tried to substantially reduce both tuition and financial aid, with mixed results. The logic of these decisions is that if tuition increases are being chased regularly by financial aid increases, then a school ought to be able to back away from both without seriously impacting the enterprise. In that way, tuition prices can more accurately reflect the real cost of the education a student receives, and a family might be able to shoulder that somewhat lower cost without massive aid and loans.

This price-/aid-slashing strategy is quite unusual and dramatic, and almost always merits much positive attention from the media. Sometimes the price-/aid-cutting strategy works quite well as designed. More students apply, and the college thrives. Sometimes, enrollment suffers, however, because not enough students choose to or just can't pay the real tuition out-of-pocket without aid.

In these cases, competing colleges who have not reduced their prices are threatened and have to justify why they are so much more expensive. They respond by striking back using the familiar "price equals quality" theme. Schools that adopt the strategy to slash tuition, their competitors argue, have been among those not perceived as being of high quality. Colleges actually characterize less-expensive schools as having lower-quality faculty, learning resources, or the like.

To understand how the school you're interested in treats its tuition costs, a study of a school's budget would be necessary to begin to understand how dollars are actually spent. Enterprises that want customers or investors are usually willing, or required, to share financial information to earn trust. Do prospective (or current) students ever request to see a budget or financial statement? Why not? It's a good indication of how your dollars will be used. See what kind of response you get.

If you do get them, these documents will be difficult to interpret. Ask for some time with a college official who can explain them to you. Rest assured your request will be much discussed behind closed doors. Most colleges have little to hide, but somehow feel that they need to do so. Certainly, individual salaries and departmental budgets can be subject for much internal campus conversation and jealousy. But as some states begin to require that the sun shine in on complex college budgeting practices, the consumer wins.

Myth 43: Financial aid decisions are based on individual student need and are blind to nonfinancial factors.

Reality: Colleges load their financial decisions to produce the kind of freshman class they want.

In the old days, financial aid directors reported to chief financial officers in order to carefully manage their budgets. But as price competition increased dramatically in the 1980s and 1990s, admissions directors properly protested that they needed more direct control over specific financial aid packaging decisions. That's when the high-tuition/high-aid strategy came of age, and when financial aid budgets began to explode on college campuses. Faced with runaway aid costs and a shotgun approach to making aid decisions, smart consultants began to realize there was a market for data-driven analyses designed to manage enrollment strategically.

The analyses intend to show colleges how to distribute their financial aid offers in order to predict and control the size, shape, and cost of the incoming class. In essence what happens is that past results in these areas are studied to predict accurately future student-applicant behavior.

Schools can target subgroups within applicant pools on almost any demographic basis. One such variable of great interest is learning how to invest aid dollars in those students most likely to be recruited for smaller discounts. High-achieving students, violinists, and quarterbacks, to pick a few subgroups, are in great demand, and it will take very large aid awards (discounts) to recruit them.

Less-attractive or -competitive applicants might be persuaded to deposit for smaller financial aid packages. It sounds compelling that this approach should reduce the aid demands on the budget by increasing net revenue. Having more students paying more of their costs out-of-pocket appears too good to be true.

Almost every school now uses some variant of this approach. One consequence of the enrollment-management model emerging in recent years is the ability to control for net revenue. The problem is that many times the strategy works too well. In addition to having consequences on the diversity and total learning environment of a campus, the ability to more easily attract students who will be willing and able to pay a larger share of the bill is an awfully seductive temptation for college administrators. More aid awards are made and accepted, class sizes swell, costs often go up when more programs and facilities are needed, and the overall effect on the budget is not as salutary as might be expected.

Moreover, decisions about the entering class based too heavily on ability to pay may easily cause some students to be turned away. You likely won't know just how much a school is assessing your financial circumstances, but if you pick up any signals that suggest they are evaluating you that way, it is OK to ask them about the variables they are using to assess your candidacy for admission. Be watching for more than a passing interest from admissions counselors about lifestyle information (e.g., what your parents do for a living, what kind of cars you or your family drive). Be especially curious if colleges seem to know these kinds of things about you even without asking. It is possible that they have purchased data about you based on statistical information available about people who live in your zip code area. Just factor in whatever you learn as you get closer to a decision and try to assess whether you are uncomfortable with colleges knowing a bit much about who your neighbors are, your political affiliations, where your family vacations or what private clubs your folks have joined.

> **Myth 44:** Academic quality issues are at the heart of how a college shapes its freshman class.
>
> **Reality:** The financial bottom line is always front and center in the mind of the college.

Ideally, you might want to believe that colleges make decisions primarily on the basis of your academic interests and ability. It is certainly true that the overwhelming majority of colleges can't and don't make a profit. They are affirmed by the IRS to be not-for-profit, and they must steadfastly justify that status each year. They pay no taxes and have no shareholders. But colleges are multimillion- or billion-dollar businesses that have to pay bills and make payroll. There is even a recent trend for some for-profit companies to get into the higher education market. It is certainly reasonable for you to inquire whether the schools you are exploring are not-for-profit. It may not make a difference in your decision making, but you might want to know how much a school's bottom-line will impact decisions about the people, programs, and physical facilities that will be available to you in college.

State institutions receive budget dollars from their legislatures that come from tax payments. For private schools, there are really only two sources of revenue: gifts, either current or the income from the investment of former gifts, and student tuition and fees.

For almost all schools, tuition is, by far, the largest and most important revenue stream. It is important to know that the few wealthy schools with endowments large enough to pay their expenses from the return on investment are the very ones who charge the highest prices, and the poorest schools often charge the lowest prices. But even at the wealthiest schools, and surely at the rest, no development office can raise enough money to keep pace with skyrocketing tuition discounts, so tuition is an essential income resource.

In the old days of college budgeting, all tuition (gross) revenue was shown as income, and financial aid tuition discounts were shown as expenses. This format failed for many reasons. For example, it made constituents believe that discounts were really dollars that might be spent for other purposes, when they were never actual dollars to be expended. The format also played havoc with formulas for calculating budget priorities because it exaggerated real income and expenses. Perhaps worst of all, it made institutions appear to be richer (i.e., have more income) than they really had.

The newer budgeting formula takes the financial aid discount as an immediate deduction from the gross tuition number to reveal the actual (net) tuition available. As schools drive up published prices for perceived quality reasons or marketing strategy, they often feel required to drive the tuition discount number and sometimes percentage higher and higher. In the 1980s, discounts of 25 percent to 33 percent were common and sustainable. More recently, we see discount percentages reaching upward of 40 percent and even 50 percent in some cases. Higher and higher tuition rates are chased by higher and higher financial aid discounts . . . this has been the pricing strategy for most colleges for the past several decades.

At first, it will seem too good to be true that you are being offered such a large discount on your tuition bill. But such practices can become out of control. There are too many examples out there of significant increases in gross tuition that have actually yielded little or no increase in net tuition, and sometimes even reductions in dollars truly available for salaries and programs. There is nothing worse for you than to be a student on a campus where a faculty member believes more money is available by looking at enrollment numbers only to discover that budgets have to be cut because of a higher-than-planned discount rate. Budget cuts will usually mean fewer services available to students.

Myth 45: All students are treated equally by the same criteria in awarding financial aid.

Reality: Admissions and financial aid directors often make individual aid decisions about how much discount is needed to convince an applicant to accept their admission offer.

In the early stages of the annual admission recruiting process, all colleges promote their programs, services, and people (i.e., "the product"). They want you to believe they have the learning opportunity most suited for your needs. As the recruiting year draws to a close, however, many colleges start to sell price, promising that they can beat the competition's costs or shave large amounts off their published price.

Many consumers have become savvy to this mode of marketing and actively comparison shop. Although educators decry such a bazaar-like quality to choosing a college, the customer in this case is in fact right. If colleges are going to try to close the sale on price, then let the customer beware and try to drive their best deal.

Numbers show that college is a good investment. College graduates earn nearly twice in a lifetime what nongraduates will make. The key is to get into a college and graduate. Although there are certainly consequences to the student for attending an elite, brand-name college versus a far less well-known, mass-market institution, most students ultimately choose between very similar schools and not between highly disparate ones. Why not then decide on the basis of the real price if there is a substantial difference? Colleges will seldom if ever publicly condone or encourage such behaviors, but their actions send a different message.

Despite ethical codes not to repackage aid awards based on other offers, schools find all sorts of creative ways to take another look once they know what other schools are offering you. Clever counselors will find "new" information that allows reconsideration. Financial aid officers will discover new awards for which applicants are eligible. Where aid based on need has been carefully analyzed, grants based on a certain talent might be brought into play. Even students and families who can afford to pay the gross tuition are influenced by small no-need grants that provide recognition. Who wouldn't want to tell a grandmother or a high school counselor about a scholarship earned? At many schools, upward of 90 percent of the entering class have at least a bit of financial aid discount impacting their final bill.

There is nothing wrong-headed or devious about these tactics designed to close a sale. They are used in many contexts in and out of education. The point is simply that each time a college makes a little decision like this, it has the net effect of increasing the gap between advertised and real price, to reduce net income, to limit a college's ability to have the extra dollars needed for instructional or other services, to increase class size, and so on. The result is that the next year the college is more likely to consider still further aggressive tuition increases exceeding the cost of living, causing political problems for colleges and—worst of all—pushing next year's aid budget still higher. So far, students and their families seem to have a high tolerance for these spiraling tuition costs. But there is not an unlimited capacity for you as a consumer to pay more and more. At some point, your choices may be restricted to more affordable colleges, and the long term health of many schools could be affected negatively for students coming along later.

Myth 46: It is important that you tell a school everything you want them to know about your financial situation.

Reality: Every school gets the same financial information about you.

Information is provided by all students in a standard way. In January of your high school senior year, you must (about the only thing regarding college you must do) file the dreaded FAFSA (Free Application for Federal Student Aid). It isn't any fun, and you will need the help of the parent(s) or person who supports you financially. You could sit with a financial aid professional and discuss all this to decide whether filing might be in your best interest. It's easier and more worthwhile to just go ahead and file the FAFSA and see what happens.

The FAFSA is available on the web (http://www.fafsa.ed.gov) and is free. Preparation and help is needed to complete this application. Some colleges now send their financial aid professionals to offer evening seminars near your location on helping prepare the FAFSA. They do this to demonstrate good faith in helping you apply—but, of course, they are hoping their efforts will sway you to think favorably about their school. And you probably should. These seminars are the kind of student-friendly, free, and convenient activity that colleges should be offering.

In filling out the FAFSA, most importantly, you and others who provide support financially must have done the federal income tax calculations for the year just ended. Since the deadline for that process isn't until April 15, this means much earlier data collection and figuring of taxes than usual for most people. But this is the only time you will have to do so, and the information is used by all schools.

The federal government uses the FAFSA to decide what it is reasonable for you and your family to pay based on your financial circumstances. There are many variables that impact what will be determined from the information provided, which is called the total family contribution. That number is provided to all schools. What they do with that information, as we shall see, varies greatly. (Note that even families with higher income and assets should take the time to fill out the FAFSA, because they might qualify for need-based aid, especially at the most expensive schools.)

Several variables greatly impact the family contribution. One major factor is the number of children in college at the same time. Another is the kind of assets a family owns. Calculations are quite technical.

After you get your results, there will be lots of time for talking, and negotiating, with financial aid folks. Every school has these professionals who have studied, and sometimes helped to shape, the complicated codes and policies that determine aid eligibility and awarding. More than anyone else on a college campus, they provide expert counseling for matters that almost no one else understands. Your admission representative will also help you and your family interpret the rules and regulations. Some colleges are now providing a financial advisor as well as an academic advisor to help with your planning. This is the kind of assistance a student-friendly campus can and should provide. Look for it!

Myth 47: Financial aid is determined by a student's need.

Reality: An increasingly large part of a college's aid budget is not based on need.

In general, colleges decide in advance roughly how much financial aid they will offer to yield a desired quantity and quality of entering students. Some of that money may actually be real dollars coming from income on the investment of what donors have provided. More often, financial aid dollars aren't real money, rather they are discounts.

Colleges play Robin Hood and take a percentage of tuition dollars paid by some and redistribute them to reduce what other students have to pay. These discount aid awards certainly go to needy students. But, often no-need or merit aid is given to students the college wants for their academic prowess or their talent, diversity, or leadership. Colleges market these discounts as scholarships to attract students to attend.

There is much discussion about how so-called average or middle-class families are caught in a squeeze financially. They cannot afford to or haven't been able or motivated to save for college costs. Or even if they have, the skyrocketing price increases have overwhelmed their planning and preparation. Although they don't have enough to pay for college themselves, they often have too much money to qualify for need-based federal and state programs.

Because there is a large number of such "squeezed" students, and colleges need to attract them to fill their ranks, schools themselves are awarding more and more of their aid budgets not on the traditional need basis but for new kinds of no-need aid. The families might actually really need the aid, but the "no-need" label comes from the fact that the students awarded fail to meet FAFSA need-based criteria.

Recently, we have witnessed more service, leadership, and extracurricular grants, often in small amounts but nevertheless helping to reduce the out-of-pocket costs to middle-class families. Top academic students have always been and will continue to be competitive for large talent financial aid awards. There is simply no other way that these students will be recruited without big grants, since they are being offered them by the competition.

However, for those students not attracting competitive attention elsewhere, the offer of a modest no-need aid package is quite helpful and tempting. Some schools have begun to recognize that these "second tier" students are numerous and available to make up the core of an entering class at a discount rate that doesn't threaten to exhaust a college's financial capacity.

Students should be eagerly looking for schools willing to help discount the cost of their education, even if they do not qualify for large talent- or need-based scholarships. Many college reference tools try to develop a measure for you to evaluate how effectively a college uses its dollars to have the greatest impact on the largest number of students possible. One such important tool rearranges quality rankings of schools based on cost. Schools with lower real costs that score fairly high in quality are likely putting most of their resources directly into people and programs that benefit students. Those are colleges that deserve your attention and respect. They are likely places where your success matters.

Myth 48: Financial aid awards are separate from the admissions process.

Reality: Financial aid gets put in a package that is offered to you as part of the "sale."

Universities don't like to admit it, but an aid award is much like an offer from a seller of any tangible property. The FAFSA tells the school what resources should come from a family, but needless to say the family may not agree. Just because the calculations say a family can pay, it doesn't mean they can or want to do so. Every individual and family has circumstances and lifestyle issues that affect ability and willingness to pay.

Regardless, the game really begins when a college tells an applicant what the actual price that needs to be paid is (as contrasted with the advertised full-tuition price). The award or financial aid package letter, usually delivered or explained by an admissions counselor, will start with the full cost of attendance (tuition, fees, perhaps room and board). It will then deduct any state or federal dollars the student qualifies for as well as institutional scholarships or grants, all the while working down toward the

FAFSA calculated family contribution. Most of the time, there are no real institutional dollars being allocated; rather, schools are discounting their published prices in an effort to recruit you.

In some cases, the net cost may be less, sometimes far less, than the family contribution. This is a case in which the student is much desired for some academic, athletic, or artistic attribute or has a very high need, that is, low family contribution. A few colleges aggressively promise that they will meet the FAFSA family contribution and never ask a student to pay more, no matter the published price. These are schools that are either wealthy enough to make up the difference and/or determined to compete effectively against other schools. Most colleges will build a package with some sort of gap between the FAFSA contribution and what they are asking you to pay. They will most likely suggest that some form of low-interest borrowing be used to help make up the difference.

Colleges use a variety of formulas they have developed to calculate the award. Variables that go into this formula include the total amount of aid dollars and discount the college has budgeted, how badly they want the particular student in question, and how far above the FAFSA family contribution they think they can afford to be and still remain competitive with other offers students will receive.

The first cut at the award letter is almost always done by a computer program loaded with the variables mentioned. There are certainly mistakes made in this stage of the process. Feel free to have a lengthy conversation with your rep or the financial aid office to be sure that what they are offering is really what they have intended. Long before negotiations might commence, you should be sure their first offer includes everything they really want you to have. It just makes good sense to have a responsible college official eyeball what the computer generated. They won't do this review automatically, given their workloads, but they will certainly think it is reasonable and will do so when requested.

Myth 49: Most aid is given as grants, not loans.

Reality: Loans are what make college affordable for most students.

You will likely read a good bit about students clever or lucky enough to have found grants, that is, "free money" to pay for much of their schooling. There are, it is true, aid dollars left unclaimed every year by students who don't realize that their parents' employers or their county of residence might offer targeted grant programs not always well publicized. But borrowing some or even all of the money to go to college is the common, economical, and good-sense method of choice for most students. Without loans, most students couldn't afford to go to college. Making loans to college students is a big business for banks and the federal government. Low-interest loans are available with friendly provisions that do not require payback until after you are in the workforce.

College financial aid offices will help you access good loans. Don't be afraid to borrow, but pay attention to some potential pitfalls. Some loans will be built into your original aid award letter based on college financial and policies. Schools vary greatly here. Be very careful, because one aid award might look better with less cost to you immediately out-of-pocket, but upon review might not be as good an offer as from another school that has you paying more immediately but has included only grants and not loans to be repaid.

One early question to ask after receiving the award letter is whether there is any flexibility in converting loans to grants, or vise versa if you are not worried about the debt burden. There are legal limits based on your FAFSA as to how much federally subsidized loan money you can borrow in any given year of your college career or in total. These are the best loans to have—banks make them with highly favorable terms because the government stands behind them.

Keep in mind there are lots of other college loan funds out there that do not require governmental support. Some of these private loans will still be better than the terms available if you just walk into a loan office off the street. Although some students do default on their loans, generally college students preparing for careers are a pretty good risk, and their parents can be asked to cosign. Ultimately, some families go outside any of the subsidized or unsubsidized loan programs available through the financial aid office and borrow money against their home equity, with other collateral, or on high-interest credit cards. Such expensive loans should be used only as an absolute last resource.

If loans are in the equation for you, and for most students they are, it is best to work closely with the experienced staff in the financial aid office to find the best deal. You may never again be in as advantaged a position to borrow money. Best of all, with federally subsidized loans and with some other private borrowing, interest may not accrue or repayment may not start until you are out of school and in the workforce, usually six or nine months after graduation. This is a remarkably good situation in which the money is costing you nothing while you are using it, and repayment is based on well-below-market interest rates and over a very long time period. Even a beginning salary can usually handle the repayment without too much difficulty.

Myth 50: College loans are smart, safe ways to pay for college.

Reality: Loans can get students and colleges in trouble.

College is a great investment and well worth borrowing money to attend, but that is true if, and only if, you graduate! The income you will likely earn as a college graduate should make it relatively easy to pay back the low-interest loans you took out to afford college. However, if you don't graduate, you will still have the loans but likely not the income. You will be paying for something you didn't get. So be sure you attend a school where you can be successful, and then make sure you succeed and graduate.

Another problem for even the successful student is borrowing too much and not always for the right reasons. College loan money is pretty easy to get and available at favorable rates. Families can borrow too much. Perhaps they haven't saved enough or don't want to change lifestyles while students are in school. Loans can pile up and saddle a family or a graduate with long-term debt, even many years after graduation. Many students graduate with $25,000 or more of college debt. If they intend to go to graduate or professional school, that amount will soar. It must be paid back along with the inevitable other borrowing for such things as a home and a car needed to start a life. A couple who meets and marries during and after college has a double payback problem, especially if both individuals have devoted themselves to meaningful careers in relatively low-paying jobs, such as teaching and nursing.

Colleges need you to borrow to make it possible for you to attend, but they also need you to repay your loans. Default rates are monitored by schools and closely scrutinized by government agencies. If a school has higher default rates than average, its ability to access government funds for future programs or financial aid may well be jeopardized, and its ratings will be negatively impacted. Sometimes even its accreditation, its right to award recognized credits and degrees, will suffer.

Sadly, there are examples of schools and individuals who try to manipulate the financial aid system. Fly-by-night colleges collect tuition from students, all of which is paid by some government program, and then they don't deliver an effective product, leaving the students with debts but not degrees. Or students try to beat the system by enrolling to access aid with no intention of ever earning a degree or paying it back. These excesses make it necessary to impose strict regulations that even honest colleges and students must deal with as well.

Saving more money for college when children are young is certainly the most efficient way to pay for an education. When most families start to think about paying the bill, it is usually too late to accumulate the savings needed. Hopefully, the experience with an older child's college costs might encourage some better preparation for future students coming along at a later date.

Remember that college, if you graduate, is an excellent investment in your future, even if you and your family haven't been able to do the best financial preparation. College is expensive, no matter how prepared you might be. Almost everyone needs and deserves some help. Financial aid officers at colleges really know their stuff. They can give you the information you need to make borrowing as safe and appropriate as possible. Find your best deal (i.e., the lowest interest rates and fairest repayment terms), don't borrow more than you absolutely need, go to college, and make sure you graduate!

Myth 51: A financial aid offer is a take-it-or-leave-it proposition.

Reality: Colleges expect you to question your aid award.

Except in cases where a student is vital to a college's profile, the initial aid award might well be a lowball offer. Dollars not spent on you can be saved for others or for different purposes. At the same time, the college certainly does not want to turn you away by presenting an embarrassingly low package, especially knowing that other schools are bidding for you as well. Your admissions counselor might well be lobbying for and consulting on what kind of package makes sense for what you are expecting and what it will take to persuade you to come. But the initial offer will likely be a figure that intends to be the lowest the college reasonably expects you to accept.

A college's ability to manage its financial budget will likely determine its overall health as an institution. The quantity and quality of the student body depends on the effective use of aid dollars. A college's sustainability demands that aid be carefully distributed and monitored. There are many examples out there of schools where the aid budget has gotten out of control. In an effort to bring in the class, too many admissions and financial aid directors have come close to giving away the store. Someone has to pay the bills. It is tempting to run up the size of the class and give an artificial feeling of momentum and good will. When the folks in the business office actually see what discount has been used to round up the entering class, there are often some very serious recriminations within the university administration. The students arrive, but the dollars to pay for their programs sometimes don't keep pace.

Although the macro aid budget is huge, it is made up of thousands of subparts representing each student's award. For most colleges, half or more of the students, sometimes upward of 90 percent, pass through the aid office. So while the total aid budget is huge and threatens the college's bottom line, each individual award must be kept as small as possible to allow the student to attend but not be excessive.

It takes a tough-minded person to say no to students and their families who really want to enroll but just can't make the cost work for them. Other students will be requesting more help. Why shouldn't you? You can't ask a college to go broke so that you can get an education. If they do, everyone, including you, will suffer. However, you can see if you can meet them somewhere in the middle financially.

For fairness, colleges have formulas to make similar aid awards to students with similar circumstances, but no two cases are ever identical. Discuss your package with your counselor. Clarify any uncertainties you have about just exactly what they are offering. When you think you and your family have the best understanding possible, request a face-to-face meeting with a high-enough-ranking admissions, financial aid, or other college official who can make or influence decisions.

Myth 52: Colleges encourage students to understand and take control of the cost of their education.

Reality: Most students don't understand and aren't prepared to discuss financial aid.

Few students ever take the time to figure out how money decisions get made. Asking good questions and understanding the process will help you a great deal. Bring your financial aid award letter with you to the meeting. If you have similar offers from other schools, bring them too. No college will openly get into a bidding war for you, but they will certainly be influenced by information about what other schools are doing.

Here are questions you want answers to in the discussion:

Is there anything that can be done to increase or augment your aid award? For example, has a campus job been figured into your package? If you have a high need (low family contribution), you and the college may be eligible for federal work-study funds if you have a campus job.

Is your award guaranteed, and if so, for how long? In some states, grants to students may not be determined until well after the aid awards have been made by colleges. What happens if the state reduces anticipated funding that you may have as part of your package? Will the college guarantee to assume whatever shortfalls may occur rather than passing them on to you? And what if the state over-funds its program? Will those extra dollars come your way to increase your award or be swallowed up by the institution?

What will happen to other scholarships or grants you may have earned from community or church groups? There are many sources of aid out there, and you would be well advised to check with your church or a social/fraternal/employer relationship you or others in your family may have. Often these groups offer specific designated aid to prospective college students. Be careful to check that if you bring such a grant, the college will let you keep it (i.e., pile it on top of the aid they have offered you). Many schools use such private grants to replace some of the aid they have offered you, the net effect of which is not to reduce your bill at all. Colleges justify such action on the Robin Hood principle that they can use the money they take back from you for other needy students. But you earned the private grant somehow, and it only seems fair that you be allowed to benefit from it.

Can the college match an aid award from another school? It is OK to ask if the college can match an aid award from another school. Only do this if you really are willing to attend the other school. Tell the aid officer you would hate to go to another campus when your heart is set on attending here. If somehow the bottom line could be made closer, you are sure that would decide to attend. Don't push for an immediate answer. Let the college think it over and get back to you. You have nothing to lose. They are not going to reduce or take back the offer they have already made. The worst you can do is to stay the same. The best is that they may let you know they can improve the aid they have offered.

Don't play this card more than once per school. Don't get into a back-and-forth bidding war, but also don't hesitate to see how far the school will go in trying to recruit you.

* * *

Myths about Other Financial College Issues

Colleges, like airlines and fast-food restaurants, are deeply engaged in cola wars. Soft-drink companies use donations, marketing, and sponsorships to get exclusive campus access to a population that drinks lots and lots of their product. If a college has Coke, it means no Pepsi is available, or vise versa. Loyal drinkers of the other brand are stuck.

Although coffee shops are making a comeback on campuses, for many students the morning (or late-night) caffeine of choice is Mountain Dew, a Pepsi product. When one campus recently went all Coca Cola, an enterprising student set up a Mountain Dew black market. He bought large quantities at the going grocery store price, transported them back to his residence hall room, and resold them to desperate fellow students at a substantial profit. A valuable lesson in free-market capitalism!

Myths 53 through 57 will help you seize opportunities other students might miss and even possibly help you invent a few new ways to make college affordable.

Myth 53: Working while going to school is a last resort.

Reality: Campus jobs are beneficial but only pay minimum wage.

There are many advantages to working on campus. Jobs are relatively easy to get without a difficult screening and interview process. Cars aren't needed to get to work. Supervisors know that academics come first and won't usually cause severe conflicts with class and study schedules. Best of all, students get to meet and know campus folks informally, and much good mentoring can occur. In fact, research often shows that having a campus job is one of the major predictors of a student's persistence to graduation.

On many campuses, student employees do much of the real work that gets things done, whether in the dish room, the library, or the maintenance crew. Campus jobs help you get to know how things happen and who makes decisions. Students develop a much greater affinity for their school when they feel a part of the team. Things go from being "them" to "us." Over time, student employees will gain experience and can become managers and leaders in the work setting. Lifetime friendships are born. These opportunities often are springboards or internships to careers that students would never have thought about before college.

Look for openings in your residence hall, in particular. Almost all student-life activities are staffed by students or very recent graduates. No child grows up wanting to be a dean of students, but college life promotes these options, and careers are made. If you really take to college life, you might never have to leave.

Financially, however, entry-level campus jobs just don't pay enough. Colleges are controlling budgets and often using federal work-study dollars that are tied to minimum-wage pay schedules. Financial aid packages often include a campus job, so working may be an obligation that doesn't put any more money in your pocket toward your expenses. Make sure you check with the school as to how a campus job will be figured into your financial aid budget.

There are opportunities but dangers in an attractive off-campus job. Study or sleep time may disappear. Interest may drift away from school toward what might be short-term benefits. Conversely, good career connections can be made off campus if the job is chosen wisely. Some contact with off-campus working people can keep a student from losing touch with the world beyond the often cloistered college community. Longer evening and weekend hours, such as at a shopping mall, might make it still possible to get your work done and even avoid some social pitfalls of wasting valuable time.

Mostly, the off-campus job provides much more competitive earning and advancement potential. Ten or twenty hours a week of off-campus earnings can really help provide money for necessary expenses. Just guard against frivolous spending that may result from working in a mall or feeling rich with a few extra dollars in your pocket.

Myth 54: A college's room and board plan is always in a student's best interest.

Reality: Colleges want to sell you their food and rent you one of their rooms.

There are very legitimate reasons to live on campus, especially in the first year. (Some schools even require that first-year students reside on campus.)

Things are easy, close, and safe. Cars aren't needed. Little energy has to be spent on ordinary everyday issues and concerns. Best of all, friends, activities, and faculty are readily available. Students can get comfortable with each other and with the campus.

Where a college is heavily residential, commuters are almost always at a significant disadvantage. Not having a place to go study, hang out, or eat is a real problem. Going to school out of one's car is not ideal. The hassles of traffic, weather, and car breakdowns get in the way of what you need to be doing. Most of all, commuters feel like outsiders with no place of their own and no access to the in-crowd conversations and culture.

Nevertheless, while prices for room and board are reasonable, they leave little room for savings. Food, in particular, costs more than it might otherwise, especially for light eaters. Most campuses set their prices knowing that not every student will take full advantage of every meal. Look for campus food programs that allow a pay-as-you-go-for-what-you-eat system rather than a one-size-fits-all comprehensive meal plan.

Some colleges offer a variety of housing options, including apartments and theme houses where several students with similar interests, for example, in a foreign language or the arts, might live and learn together. Some of these options allow for less-expensive meal plans since students may have some cooking options not available in a residence-hall setting.

After a year or two on campus, some students find it a benefit to move off campus. Living in the community can teach responsibility and, if costs are shared, can be financially attractive. By this time, you will know what is what on campus and can easily float back and forth between your former on-campus residential life and your new independent living. College juniors and seniors often have much more customized schedules requiring off-campus travel to experiential learning in community schools, hospitals, or offices. Student teachers and nurses often need to be up and out earlier than a campus culture, which tends to stay up late and start slowly in the morning.

An idea gaining popularity is for a student's family, if possible, to buy a relatively inexpensive house near the campus where student housing tends to be readily available and affordable. By renting space in the house to other classmates, a student can sometimes make money on housing, or at least live rent-free. After graduation the house can be sold to another student family (the demand is always there), and you might even make a profit. Just be careful. When you rent to others, you become a land-lord, and sometimes that can lead to problems. You certainly won't want to deal with the hassles or responsibilities that come with late rent payments, excessive property damage, underage drinking, or other issues.

Myth 55: These days, students should take five or six years to earn a degree.

Reality: You can do it in fewer than four.

The longer you take to graduate, the more it will cost you. Don't unnecessarily delay your progress toward graduation. You came to get the degree, so work diligently at that goal.

Some schools will limit your financial aid to four years even though they know the systems they have put in place may require longer to finish. The federal government gives you only ten semesters of aid eligi-bility. Students close to graduation are certainly going to do whatever it takes to finish, given the investment they have already made. Aid is used to recruit students and retain them early in their careers. Later on, colleges know they can back off aid to veteran students without losing them. Be sure to question colleges about what you need to do guarantee that your aid award will serve you well all the way to graduation.

Even more important, see to it that you graduate on time or early. Sometimes it makes sense to stay a little longer to earn another degree, finish a second major or certificate, have an excellent internship, or improve your package of skills and experiences. But usually if you are diligent, you can make sure you graduate on time, or early!

You can earn credits any number of inexpensive ways. Use them all. Take and complete high school advanced-placement classes. See what college classes you can place out of because of your proficiencies. Take college overloads, where you pay a reduced rate for the extra hours. Go to inexpensive community colleges for summer classes. (Make sure in advance that these will transfer back to your school; the registrar or dean can tell you.) When you get close to finishing, especially if you have a good off-campus job or internship, drop down from full-time to part-time student status.

You will pay a lot less. You might lose some financial aid, but run the numbers to see if it benefits you in the end to do so. The lower hourly tuition rate for part-time students almost always makes it worthwhile.

You can probably save a semester or even a year by using some or all of these tactics without sacrificing the quality of your education. Not only will you save thousands of dollars of tuition money, but you can also get into the job market that much sooner, even if you have graduate or professional school in your plans.

By the way, you can extend the start date for repayment of most student loans if you continue your formal education after college. And there are beginning to be some programs and employers who will help you repay those loans if you promise to go to work for them for a period of time. As baby boomers retire, college graduates will be more and more in demand and can negotiate ways to pay for college. In high-demand fields, such as nursing, see if a hospital will underwrite the cost of schooling if you promise them a few years of post-graduation employment.

Myth 56: It is always best to enroll as a freshman at the school you want to graduate from later.

Reality: You can still go to the college of your choice after a year or two at a community college.

There are lots of good reasons to go to the same college for all of your undergraduate education. Academic programs are designed to take you from start to finish, and they are never quite as good if you only go part-way. But if you can't afford four years at an expensive place, maybe you can make two or three years there work almost as well for you.

The reality of current college experience is that most students transfer, and often more than once. Colleges don't talk about or market this transfer option. Why should they? They want all of you (and your money) for educational and financial reasons. Yet they also know that a significant number of their students will leave before they graduate and that they need, if possible, to replace these folks. That's where the transfer market becomes important.

Schools in big cities, in particular, will find that many local high school graduates depart for far away places only to return home after a semester or a year, in search of a local option.

All states now have some kind of inexpensive community/junior college availability. Introductory classes in these schools are certainly acceptable in transfer for programs at most universities. Often two- and four-year colleges articulate, that is, they broker in advance how their classes fit together in a student's interest.

There are academic and personal reasons to start at a community college. You might improve your study habits in a somewhat less competitive and challenging environment. You can start college really close to home if it will be a hard transition to cut loose from the safe and familiar world you have known.

There are also powerful financial incentives. Transferring out of a two-year college can happen at any point, up to and including earning an associate's degree. That degree may especially help because some four-year schools will grant automatic junior status if you bring an associate's degree with you. In essence, they waive all freshman and sophomore requirements. Check out in advance how the college of your choice will handle credits and degrees you are bringing with you. If these are managed carefully, you might cut your college bill nearly in half.

A variant of the community college savings route would be to attend a less-expensive public four-year school for the first year or two then transfer to a more expensive private school. Or, since the expensive places often have excellent freshman-year programs, you might think about getting a great jump start at the private school of your choice before transferring to a less-expensive, large state university where specialized junior- and senior-year training is often emphasized. It makes sense to do your work in the academic environment that is focused on where you are in the process. Intense mentoring, available at small private colleges, is usually a great help when getting started. Students don't often need their hands held as much as they move toward completion of their degree work. Large universities will often be better suited to advance your specialized graduate school or career planning and therefore a better choice for the later stages of your college education.

Myth 57: A student has few options in the complicated world of finances and financial aid.

Reality: You can take control of how to make college affordable just as you can take control of where and how you will earn your degree.

The central message is always the same: Colleges like to hold all the cards and control how students advance through the system. That model works for them since they have large organizations to manage.

For you as a student, the college's control is the worst way for you to make decisions, grow, and learn. Life and careers require independent thinking that must be practiced. Start applying these skills very early. Take control of how you will make college affordable. You can do it. You can graduate without crushing debt burdens. It will allow you many more future options about how you choose to live and work. In addition, you will know that you did it for yourself, which is the best feeling and lesson of all.

- **Understand everything you can about how a college operates its finances.**
  Students almost never know, so this will put you head and shoulders above everyone else.
- **Make sure you file all necessary information that is required of you in a timely and orderly manner.**
- **Don't pass on opportunities because you are unprepared.**
  That's the most common way financial aid dollars are left on the table where you can't spend them.
- **Study that financial aid award.**
  Ask questions. These matters are often kept over-complicated to discourage you from challenging what is included.
- **Figure out what you need to make things work financially and then go ask for it!**
  If you don't ask, you won't get!
- **Make a budget and stick to it.**
  Accept no credit card offers!
- **Work while you are in college.**
  Figure out where you have extra time and put it to work for you by taking a part-time job or doing things that will generate dollars (baby-sitting, yard work, etc).

- **Find housing and food options that suit your lifestyle.**
  Don't settle for one-size-fits-all plans.
- **Keep that troublesome car at home.**
  Ride a bike and you will save the time spent at the gym.
- **Get creative.**
  Start a business while in school. Maybe you will be the next David Packard (Hewlett Packard, or HP) or Bill Gates (Microsoft).

By taking control and being proactive about how you pay for your college education, you may very well learn more than in a first-year class on economics. You will decode mystical things such as loans and interest. You will discover how to be a renter and even a landlord. In an on-campus or off-campus job, you will become familiar with business practices, record keeping, and supply and demand. Punctuality, appearance, courtesy, and customer service will become habits.

The process of how things get done financially will be the greatest teacher of all. Not to mention, you will be a giant step closer to earning that college degree, armed with which you can apply all that you have learned and make everything you had to do to get there worthwhile.

Myths about Making the Decision and Preparing for School

Many colleges host events where admitted students come to campus and get a chance to stay in a residence-hall room with a current student. Apparently, at one school, instructions weren't too clear in the promotional materials about what parents were supposed to do while their child stayed on campus. One student arrived with her mother, and when the student was assigned to a room, the mother then asked which room she would be staying in for the night. The mother was told that the Holiday Inn would probably be a better choice for her. She had thought she was going to experience campus life firsthand as well.

Myths 58 through 65 walk you through the dos and don'ts of the final stages of your decision-making process. You have gotten yourself ready to make an easy, informed choice. There should be few surprises at this stage.

Myth 58: It all comes down to April 1 and May 1.

Reality: Many admissions decisions get made on a "rolling" basis all through the year.

As we have seen, the policies of the handful of elite, highly selective colleges tend to influence the standard for the many, many other American higher educational institutions. Nowhere is the power of this control more visible than in the long-standing policy that all applicants will be informed of their admissions decisions on April 1 and must announce their intentions no more than thirty days later, by May 1.

On April 1 the envelopes arrive in the mail at home to great fanfare and trepidation. Thicker is usually better than thinner since acceptances come with lots of paperwork to be returned. Colleges have had student applications since the first of the year or before. Now they are offering students a much shorter time frame to make their decisions and in an extremely busy time at the end of the high school senior year. If you have been accepted at several colleges, you must analyze all the information you receive, including financial aid packages, and revisit your top choices to tie up loose ends.

Fortunately, if you have applied to a variety of schools, some will have made you aware of their decision much earlier in the year. This is so helpful and friendly to students. You have time to sort things out better. Colleges can roll their admissions decisions through the first four months of the calendar year. If a student file is complete, many colleges can get a decision made and inform you about it in less than a month. Furthermore, prior to April 1, they can send you a financial aid award. These packages are sometimes delayed because colleges must wait for the federal government to process all the FAFSA information and send it to the financial aid office.

No matter when colleges let you know of their decision, they do respect the May 1 date for the news about where you plan to attend. Of course, you can tell them sooner, and that information is useful for everyone's planning. However, it is student friendly to wait for May 1, when all possible information can be gathered and processed.

Your admission representatives can really be helpful at this most critical stage. Remember, they will be eager to motivate you to accept their offer, but the good ones will be patient and understanding. If May 1 approaches and you aren't ready to decide, especially if you are still waiting for information rather than just confused, don't hesitate to ask for a brief extension. In fact, in the sections ahead we will explore a variety of ways in which you could, and perhaps should, continue to test your decision for a while longer.

Colleges do need to know who is planning to attend. There is important preparation for all concerned during the summer. But this college choice may be the most important adult decision you have made so far, and you shouldn't have to make it under pressure as if you had a gun to your head.

Myth 59: Colleges will find you a nuisance and unsure of yourself if you keep coming back before you have decided where to enroll.

Reality: You can't visit enough. Trying on the experience is essential.

Your first visit months ago was just to get a feeling, an impression to help decide whether to apply. It was a very low-risk situation. You really didn't know if the college even would admit you should you apply.

Now you know where they stand: They want you as a student. You have been admitted. Don't get a big head about it, but you should feel proud and in the driver's seat. For the first time, finally, you have the control.

Go back to each school you are now seriously considering. Stay for at least a day and overnight. Your high school work missed isn't as important as what you will learn on the visit.

The college will likely pair you up with a host. If not, request one, preferably someone in classes and activities that are close to your own interests.

Shadow your host to at least a few classes. Soak it up. Try to get a good feel for the atmosphere in the classroom, laboratory, or gymnasium. What vibes are you getting from students? Ask questions. Does it feel comfortable for your learning style?

You will probably have an appointment with a professor in the field you have indicated as a possible major. Are there students and faculty interacting in the office? Is there a quiet, informal place where these conversations are encouraged? Check out the library, the computer labs, and the health center too. Does everything seem in order?

Have a meal. They will certainly provide that for free. Can you see yourself having two or three meals a day for thirty weeks in the cafeteria? See what students are doing for recreation: Do they play sports, hang out in the student center, or watch movies?

Probably the biggest test is the night in the residence hall. You probably haven't been on a campus after dark. Do students feel safe? Do you? Are people moving about comfortably? What's the atmosphere on the hall floor? Are there quiet hours?

There are no right and wrong answers for all these questions. You are trying on the experience to see how it makes you feel. It will be a bit unnatural because, hard as you try, you still do not belong there yet. Even so, comparisons among the few schools you are still considering should come readily. Not all environments suit all students. This is your chance to figure out what is best for you. It is impossible to be 100 percent sure, and there are other experiences just ahead for you to continue to validate your decision.

The most important question for you is still the same. Where do you think you can be most successful? In the end, that's all that really matters.

Myth 60: You must finally make your decision by May 1.

Reality: May 1 is just the day on which deposits become nonrefundable—maybe.

Whenever you receive the good news that you have been accepted to a college, you will be expected to pay a deposit if you want to reserve your spot in the entering class. Usually the amount for the deposit is a few hundred dollars that will be applied against your account when you become a student. That's a significant amount of money, but not a great deal when you figure that you will be paying thousands of dollars someplace eventually for a college education. Even better, if you decide later not to enroll, any deposit paid at any college is 100 percent refundable prior to May 1.

Colleges want you to believe that paying the deposit is a final decision to enroll, and, in fact, very few requests for deposit refunds occur. But let's think about the deposit situation a bit longer.

Hopefully, you will be ready on or before May 1 to make your decision and move ahead through the summer with the vital final preparations to enroll. You certainly don't want to wait until after May 1 to pay your deposit, since that may well mean your spot in the entering class could be given to someone else perhaps now on a waiting list. However, if you still want more time or information, you have a couple of options, never advertised, to delay a final decision. (By the way, if you do get wait listed at a college of your choice, don't despair. Proceed with other options, but play it out with the college making you wait. Others will turn down offers, and you might still get in.)

One option is to simply ask the places that have accepted you to extend the deadline to hold your spot without a deposit (or with a still refundable deposit) beyond May 1. Colleges make the rules, so they can bend them if they want to do so. Don't expect a long extension, but two weeks might be possible. If they turn down this request, you haven't lost anything, and you might have learned something valuable about their willingness to help you make your choice.

Your best option (and it might cost some dollars but not near as much in the long run as making a bad decision) is to pay more than one deposit, even knowing you might not get some back. Cut the schools you are seriously considering to a precious few, preferably no more than two. If you genuinely need more information, pay what colleges call multiple deposits. They know some students will do this. You have now literally bought yourself all the time you need through the summer since both schools expect that you are coming.

It will get a little crazy and busy to genuinely act as if you are planning to start at both places, but the best way to really know how you will be treated as a student is to see what happens after the colleges think you have said yes. Does the treatment change when they are no longer actively recruiting you? How do you feel about the classes you will take, the faculty with whom you will work, and the activities and living circumstances available?

> **Myth 61:** Summer orientation isn't important.
>
> **Reality:** No matter what you have to sacrifice, go to summer orientation!

Almost all colleges invite students who have paid deposits, and usually their parents as well, to a summer-orientation session held in the first few weeks after high school graduations. The principal purpose of this event is to have students register for their first semester of classes. Included as well in the time on campus are placement tests, financial aid seminars, housing tours, activity and campus employment fairs, and general information sessions.

Summer orientation is among the most important steps in the whole college-search process: It prepares those students who are absolutely sure of their decision for the start of school; it solidifies decisions for some students who are still a little shaky about their choice; and it usually helps students still waffling between two schools to make up their minds. This day (or sometimes day and overnight) on campus is a perfect chance to really try on college life in a still relatively risk-free way. When summer orientation is over, there will be six or eight weeks back in normal life at home before college starts in earnest. So whatever has to be done to ensure you get to summer registration, do it, and convince a parent or both, if possible, to accompany you. The work, ballgame, or socializing missed at home can be made up much more easily than the experience gained on campus.

Furthermore, most colleges offer multiple opportunities throughout a several-week period to attend summer orientation. Sign up for one of the earliest sessions, preferably the first. All colleges operate their student class advising on a seniority basis. The number of spaces available in most sections of classes is usually limited, and next fall's college seniors, juniors, and sophomores have already registered during the previous spring college term.

Fortunately for first-year students, their more veteran student peers are not usually competing for seats in the primarily introductory classes that most new students take. However, space in introductory classes is not unlimited, and those classes and professors judged to be most popular by the powerful campus grapevine will fill up quickly in the first few summer registration sessions.

Effective colleges take pains to protect as many spaces and available faculty as possible for their new students, but classes often close before the end of summer registration. You don't want just the leftovers available if you show up toward the last of the sessions. Besides, colleges have figured out that their better, more-aware entering students will be savvy to the trick of getting to an early summer-registration session. Schools will be sure to put their best feet forward in these earliest sessions and have their most talented, energetic people on hand if at all possible. For the same money, so to speak, you can get the best service at the first or second advising period in the summer.

Myth 62: One size fits all when it comes to introductory first-year classes.

Reality: There are many ways to customize first year classes, if you look for them.

It's almost a cartoon-like stereotype that first-year college students sit in large, impersonal sections of introductory this and general that. To be sure, most colleges expect that at the beginning, students will take classes that prepare them for college in general and for their specialized fields of study in particular. As students progress through their careers into more advanced work, it is likely that more personalized, smaller classes will come along.

There are more than a few grains of truth in this common understanding of new-student academic experiences. The overwhelming majority of students who do not succeed to graduation leave college during or just after their first year. Of these students who leave disappointed, almost all get off to a bad start. Most colleges make a fatal mistake in assuming that new students will just grin and bear a kind of college trial by fire in the first year or semester. Missteps at first can spiral quickly downhill as students lose what little confidence they may have brought with them.

It doesn't have to be this way. Colleges with much higher graduation rates among their students really work at frontloading quality experiences into the first semester of the first year of study. A good start almost always guarantees success and persistence to graduation. You have worked hard to find this kind of potential success in college, and summer registration is the place where it all begins, as faculty advisors and students collaborate to outline a path toward graduation.

A few suggestions for getting started might be useful. You will likely enroll in three to five classes. Many colleges provide, and some require, at least one first-semester smaller class or seminar where students work on skills that will help them be successful. If such a class is offered, even as an elective (not required), choose it. That guarantees a few times a week when you will know your instructor and peers on a more personal basis.

If your college offers it, and you are eligible, take a close look at honors work. These will be smaller classes with other excellent students and usually motivated faculty who enjoy teaching them. Having these classes on your record (colleges call that a transcript) should also help later with graduate and professional school admissions.

Also, take any and all placement tests offered at summer orientation or other times. These instruments are no-risk opportunities. You can't start below the entry level in fields such as mathematics, writing, and foreign language, but your testing might show that you can place out of or above the usual first class in a field. That will get you going rapidly and often in smaller classes with more advanced students. If you have done advanced-placement work in high school, make sure the college gives you credit, which has the same effect of moving you ahead quicker toward graduation.

Myth 63: College faculty don't really want to teach introductory students.

Reality: At some schools if you try hard, you can find some who do!

If you are using summer orientation to make your final decision, the kind of class schedule you can build with the person assigned to be your advisor should help a great deal in clarifying your college choice. How it feels to work with that faculty person will likely be the factor that finally cements your decision. If you are already firmly decided, this beginning relationship with an advisor is also very important in coaching you on how to be successful in your new college home.

Faculty are often rewarded for doing research, publishing their findings, and teaching advanced students. Not many schools place a high priority on senior professors spending time with entering students. If you find one that does, sign up to enroll if they will have you. A few schools have figured out that if they really want new students to be successful, they should put their best, most experienced teachers with them.

Some of the professors working at summer orientation may be these good, or great, teachers. They may have been asked by the college to help advise, or they might be so dedicated that they have volunteered. Most college faculty are under contract for the nine months of the typical academic year from late August through mid-May. They value their summer time and aren't paid much for coming back to do extra duty like summer registration.

If you are lucky, your summer advisor may be your full-time advisor when school starts in the fall. That's probably not the case, however, since there are far fewer professors available in the summer. Still, you can begin to get a flavor for how college faculty think and operate. You will probably have some group time with the professor and the other students assigned to this person and then an individual appointment of at least thirty minutes during which you will actually select your classes.

Years after graduating, most college alumni report they cannot remember much or anything specific that they learned in a particular class. Yet they all remember a few of their instructors. It is the people you study with, at least a few of them, who will shape your collegiate experience and memories. They will make you mad and sad. You will try to figure them out. Their habits of the mind and of the heart will cause you to think about things in all new ways. In the best cases, these professors become more than advisors; they become colleagues and mentors and friends.

You should sense even in the brief time you spend with a summer advisor that a new kind of relationship is developing from the ones you had even with your favorite high school teachers. You might not know much as a new college student, but four years later you will be expected to think and work independently. By nurturing you and challenging you, college faculty should move you through the transition toward this independence. If you feel that process beginning at the time you are selecting classes for the fall, it may be a little scary, but know you are in the right place, and your decision to attend should be easy and feel right.

Myth 64: Extracurricular activities are just to pass the time and pad your resume.

Reality: The best lessons are often learned outside of class in college.

Students come to college to take classes that result in earning degrees, but the experiences and skills that best prepare graduates for their futures often happen when students are not in class.

From time to time, these out-of-class opportunities are called "extra" or "co" curricular, or sometimes the "second curriculum," meaning that they are informal but planned learning activities. They happen in any of the other places on campus (e.g., residence hall, student center) when students are not in class.

A significant part of summer orientation will introduce new students to such activities. More than most students realize, and more than some colleges know, the time spent writing for the student newspaper or serving as student government treasurer or competing on the debate team may determine college success. All student outcome research points to the importance of being involved. The most successful graduates appear to have five or six meaningful involvements with campus life during their college years. Many college campuses are havens for personal safety and intellectual discovery. There are few places or opportunities after college to try things out in such a low-risk environment.

Sometimes students grow edgy at what they might describe as the bubble or cloister they live in on campus, where real-world issues might not interfere. Activities such as service learning through community or international outreach help to bring the campus and the world together. It is virtually impossible to find a student who has studied abroad, for example, who has not seen that time spent in another culture as life-changing. Seeing the world through someone else's eyes may be in fact a functional definition of what it means to be college educated.

Even at non-church-related colleges, you don't have to check your faith at the campus gate and pick it back up again after graduation. Almost all campuses have activities where the spiritual dimension of human experience can be explored. College sharpens the critical-thinking powers of the mind. Out-of-class religious life activities can strengthen values awareness as well.

Some students arrive with well-developed environmental concerns. Eco-consciousness can provide a powerful co-curricular focus. Campuses certainly benefit from becoming greener. There are abundant examples of student-led conservation activities that have made colleges healthier and have started careers for graduates.

In making your final college choice and in preparing to get off to a fast start once you arrive, closely check out the activities described at summer orientation. There should be energetic staff and students available to share their enthusiasm with you. If you don't see something to your liking, find out how easy it may be to start a new club or activity that may appeal to others. The leadership opportunities gathered in trying to get something off the ground may be the most valuable part of college life. Bring your unique set of interests and experiences with you to the benefit of all concerned.

Test and retest your feelings and expectations about extracurricular options. Go to activities fairs associated with summer orientation, ask current students about where they choose to be involved, chat with staff and faculty sponsors of the clubs and teams you think you might like. If it feels like you can make a difference here, then you have almost certainly found the right place to go to college.

Myth 65: Residence-hall life is tough and just to be endured.

Reality: There are many, many options when it comes to living on campus, and some are pretty nice.

Residence halls used to be called dormitories, as in places people sleep, and there are lots of jokes about them. Every campus still has the old-fashioned high-rise-style buildings with slow, small elevators, two students to a tiny room, narrow hallways, and group showers. New students tend to experience these older facilities because these are the rooms most frequently available as veteran students have opted out to newer campus housing as soon as they can.

Most colleges have tried to spruce up these older residence halls to make them safer, more hospitable and more equipped to carry the electronic load given all the technology that today's students bring along. You probably won't be able see the room assigned to

you since campuses host a variety of summer events
that require housing, or maintenance and custodial
work may be happening during the summer downtime. However, some of the halls will be available for
viewing during summer orientation, so be sure to
take a peek. You might be able to meet the hall
director—probably a recent graduate rather than
the matronly housemother of yesteryear. Maybe the
resident assistant, a current student who will be
paid a bit and get reduced or free housing to live on
the floor with you and provide some minimal supervision, might be part of the student-orientation
corps working summer orientation.

Even for new students there may be some other
options available. Colleges that care about success in
persistence to graduation have created a broad
range of housing stock to meet the demand of more
consumer-conscious students. These spaces will be
your home for one to four years, so residence life
does matter.

Honors colleges, to attract top students, sometimes offer "living-learning" floors with enhanced
amenities and quiet hours. Sometimes rooms, suites,
or even entire halls with these enhancements are
available at somewhat higher prices. Suites, in fact,
are an alternative to the traditional two to a room.

They offer more space and sometimes have a spot for a new student or two. Having some experienced roommates is often a valuable way to gain insights and ready-made friendships.

See if there are any theme-house spaces still available. These are small houses in the campus neighborhood owned by the college and used to house a few students with common interests. The best of these houses are where students all studying the same foreign language, for example, might live and eat together, often with a graduate student from the country in question, providing an immersion-like experience without leaving home.

Schools have recently been building nice apart-ment complexes on campus to try to keep students from moving off to the many private apartment buildings that crop up nearby. These units house three or four students who usually know each other and have signed up during the previous school year. Sometimes a space or even a room for two pops up in these buildings during the summer because of changed circumstances for students who thought they were going to live there. Keep an eye out for such listings at orientation.

You probably won't make your college choice on the basis of housing options available, but you certainly should be able to feel your residence hall experience won't get in the way of your success, and might even help.

Start making your shopping list and thinking about move-in arrangements. The hour is fast approaching when everything you have done leads to what is now an easy, obvious choice of the right place for your college career.

MYTHS ABOUT LAST-MINUTE PREPARATIONS BEFORE STARTING

Colleges expect payment either at the beginning of each semester or in accordance with established payment plans, sometimes monthly during the school year. One parent, skilled in the ways of cash management and with some extra dollars in pocket, called a college chief financial officer in May of his child's high school graduation. "Since I don't have to pay you for several months, and since you are probably tight for cash in the summer before tuition is due and might need to borrow at going rates like 6 percent, why not let me pay my bill now, giving you some needed cash, and you give me a 3 percent discount so we all win." The chief financial officer jumped at the offer of below-market cash, and the family saved a few hundred bucks.

Morale of the story: Creativity and imagination matter, and not just when it comes to money. If the offer had been rejected, no harm would have been done. Don't be afraid to ask for what you want!

No two undergraduate careers, even in the same school with the same major, are ever identical. Myths 66 through 69 should help you think about ways to make college not just something you experience passively but something you invent for yourself in an active way. The lasting lessons you will learn will most likely come more from what you do for yourself rather than from what you are taught by others.

Myth 66: When it comes to a roommate, you just have to hope for the best.

Reality: You can control your roommate situation, within reason.

By the end of summer orientation, you should be able to make your final college choice if you haven't already. Be alert that surprises might still materialize as you go through the last few weeks before school starts, and there is always the chance you might need to rethink your decision. That does happen from time to time. Be professional and courteous with schools you are rejecting, especially with the one that might have come in as a second choice. If you get in a real bind, you might need to reopen conversation with that college.

One issue that causes some consternation at the start of school or early in the year is roommate compatibility. Colleges will try to collect information from new students and use it to match roommates, but this is an imperfect science at best. For a long time, schools tried to keep smokers and nonsmokers apart, but most campuses have declared all their buildings smoke-free now, so that issue is moot. Smoking aside, there are all kinds of reasons, just as in any living relationship, where roommates have potential conflicts. In the confined space of a college residence hall, the major lightning-rod issues usually have to do with alcohol, schedules, noise, neatness, and significant others spending too much time in the room.

Conflict resolution is a part of the learning environment at a college, and school officials will help roommates to work out their issues peacefully. There are some ways to prepare to minimize difficulties in advance before they get out of hand. Even though most restrictive behavior rules that may have existed a generation ago are now gone, campuses still usually offer to women, at least, the chance to live in single-sex residence halls. For some people, this works better at reducing distractions. Some residence halls or at least floors within a residence hall also operate like self-governing democracies wherein policies are established for all concerned, thereby minimizing the source of much one-on-one conflict.

Some students who already know each other and are headed to the same college prearrange to live together. This can work out very well, although even friendships sometimes fade when two people haven't previously shared the same space. Also college is about trying new things and meeting new people, so if roommates are too close, it might get in the way of learning.

To prepare for living with your roommate, what probably works best is to get the name and contact information for your soon-to-be roommate and communicate in advance as much as seems reasonable. Decisions can be made about who brings what.

In time maybe even lifestyle issues can be broached before you are sharing a ten-by-twelve space in the middle of the night during midterm exam week.

Sometimes students even pay a substantial amount extra to get a single room that they don't have to share. Colleges offer a few of these. For advanced students, a single room might make a lot of sense. Some people become resident assistants just to get a room to themselves. For new students, roommates, despite whatever issues have to be worked out, are usually a good thing. College life can be lonely and stressful. Being too alone may not be in your best interest.

Myth 67: Athletics is a world unto itself on a college campus.

Reality: At most schools, athletics is an important part of the student experience.

The most famous, visible, largest universities operate big-time athletic programs with tens of millions of dollars at stake. The remarkably gifted athletes who participate in undergraduate sports competition at this nearly professional level are certainly a breed apart on most campuses. The great majority of such athletes choose to or are forced to put their team above their academic careers, and very many of them never graduate on time or, sadly, at all.

Yet for every nationally elite athletic program that commands all the media attention, there are at least fifty schools where student athletes participate in sports competition that is well balanced with classroom pursuits. As you prepare to be successful in college, consider whether you might want to pursue participation on a team.

Top high school athletes will be recruited by college coaches. The best of them will be offered full or partial athletic scholarships. Even some nonelite athletic programs offer financial assistance reserved for athletes. The National Collegiate Athletic Association as well as college sports conferences and the programs themselves carefully monitor rules designed to eliminate unfair competition and to protect students from abusive practices. But the majority of college athletes participate in nonscholarship programs or are walk-ons without a scholarship or "ride."

Besides the major college sports of football and basketball, there are minor team sports and lots of individual opportunities in programs such as golf, tennis, and track and field. Although preoccupation with any activity can get in the way of classroom success, many intercollegiate varsity athletes at the less-celebrated programs have strong records of academic and leadership performance. Coaches need players to maintain adequate grade point averages and satisfactory progress toward graduation, so they encourage attendance and preparation in the classroom. Sports participation requires conditioning, which tends to enhance health and discipline that can benefit students, who might otherwise eat poorly, drink too much, or not get enough rest. Managing time and minimizing distractions, as most athletes must, also keep students focused on what they need to do and not waste time on frivolous activities. A sense of teamwork provides ready-made friendships, helps students relate better on the many collaborative projects they need to complete in class, and certainly gets a graduate ready for the world of work.

At best, walk-on players at schools with scholarships may perform well enough to earn some financial assistance for doing what they enjoy anyway. Athletic success gives a new student a sense of pride, a feeling of belonging to a community, a greater visibility that may feel good, and a chance to keep family and hometown friends connected to the college experience. At some colleges more than 25 percent of all full-time students participate in undergraduate varsity athletics. For male students, the number is often even higher.

If organized athletics is not of interest or out of reach, consider, at least, taking a look at a school's intramural sports options. These programs are for fun and conditioning only, have many of the same benefits as the varsity competition, and are available to all students. The social life of a college, especially in the cold winter months on many campuses, is often built around the late evening tussles on the basketball or volleyball courts of an indoor recreational facility. Often these programs, usually co-ed, allow you to work off some study stress or some calories from the cafeteria, to make new friends from other parts of the campus, to see faculty and staff in a very different setting, or even to find a date for formal.

Myth 68: Having fraternities and sororities on campus is either a good or bad thing depending on how they are managed by the college.

Reality: A Greek system is always a mixed blessing for the campus and the students.

Almost no one you will talk with is neutral about the value (or lack thereof) of fraternities and sororities. Whether you join or not can dramatically shape your whole college experience. Unfortunately, if your campus has a Greek system, you will likely have to make this decision very early and without adequate information.

Not all schools have fraternities and sororities, and their presence or absence may have impacted your college choice. Perhaps you are a "legacy" in that a parent or sibling was an active member in the past, perhaps being an independent is something you are convinced about, or perhaps you haven't made up your mind yet.

Some Greek systems are weak, with few members and without their own housing. If that's the case, a decision to join or not probably won't make much of a difference. However, where there is a powerful system with many Greek houses and more than half the student population belonging, the decision easily determines your social life and friendships.

These heavily Greek campuses often hold early rush, where new students have to decide if they want to consider membership when school starts in the fall or even before. At some of these places, where the fraternities and sororities house so many students, the university may have made little investment in their own housing. At these places, students often move right into the Greek houses even while they are going through a pledge period before they are initiated as full members. A few schools have delayed or deferred rush until second semester to give all students a few months to gather information. Sometimes this reform doesn't work because Greek organizations engage in what's called "dirty rush," when they contact students before the official open period for such invitations is authorized.

At many schools, all new students must spend the first year in college-owned residence halls even after they have become members of the Greek houses. It is hoped that this uniform first-year housing experience for independents and students interested in fraternities/sororities will breed some friendships that will last and bring students closer together rather than separate them. In reality, once students pledge and join fraternities and sororities, they spend so much time with their "brothers and sisters" that friendships with independents become difficult to sustain.

In confidence, most college people can tell you the reasons why you should and should not join. Fraternity and sorority members will likely be friends for life, supporting each other in college and after. Students in the Greek system on most campuses are the active student and later alumni leaders. Fraternity and sorority houses are usually the center of a campus social life. Good grade point averages are required for initiation, and so the houses encourage student academic success.

On the other hand, there is often intense peer pressure from brothers and sisters to rush, pledge, and become actives. Social conformity can result, and sometimes students are rejected or "black-balled" with an inevitable social stigma and pain resulting. Greek houses often witness rampant alcohol and sexual abuse. Fraternity and sorority files of previous class tests and papers may make academic dishonesty too tempting.

All you can do to prepare yourself for this critical choice is to find out as much you can about the pros and cons and then make the best informed decision that works for you. One suggestion would be to go through rush, difficult as it may be so early in your time on campus, and then decide for yourself if you feel Greek life will help you succeed. As in all things regarding college, make your progress toward successful graduation the ultimate criterion. With that core value in mind, you will likely make the right choice.

Remember that if you decide to go ahead with a fraternity or sorority and things don't turn out the way you hoped, you can always depledge or deactivate. That decision will be difficult for a while, but there will be few if any permanent consequences, and certainly not as many as staying in the system if it isn't working for you. The reverse mode is more difficult, but once in a while if you said no to being Greek in your first year, it may be possible to be considered as a sophomore or even a junior if that appears attractive to you later—based on gaining more firsthand information.

Myth 69: It's best to wait until you move in to buy books, computers, and other supplies.

Reality: There is neither a foolproof time nor method to acquire what you need.

Colleges will make everything you need readily available in the summer or during move-in just before classes start. They want to make it easy for you, and they make money on just about everything you buy. Auxiliaries, as they are called (such as room, board, and bookstore), are an important part of a college's revenue.

Buying books on campus is convenient, especially if problems arise and you might need to return or exchange. However, book lists are almost always available during the summer for all classes, although it might take a little digging to get them. Textbooks are a major, if sometimes hidden, cost. Colleges and the government do factor books and supplies into the legitimate expenses of your education for financial aid packaging purposes, but it always seems more expensive than you expect.

New textbooks can easily cost more than $100. Most of this money goes to the publisher. Authors and bookstores make surprisingly little from the sales. New editions come out frequently, in part to keep up with current knowledge and just as much to make used books antiquated. There is a brisk business in buying and selling used texts, although students seem to make very little when they sell their texts back and pay a premium when they buy used editions. Bookstores can be caught in a bind buying used texts and then discovering that professors are changing their required reading lists for next semester. Used book companies make the rounds on college campuses buying up used texts to sell at other colleges where they might be used. These middlemen offer very little money for the books they buy, but often sellers have no other choice. Professors sometimes sell free desk copies of texts they receive in the mail for possible classroom adoption. The whole college book business is a messy proposition for all concerned.

Some campuses, usually inspired by student cooperatives, try to eliminate the many hands that profit and add cost to the book exchange business. These book co-ops arrange to put student sellers and buyers together. Sometimes enterprising individual students will take the initiative to list all over campus or on the college's computer network the books they wish to sell. Or armed with the book lists, you can go out to the various used book stores and websites to find your best deal.

Almost every college student today needs and has access to a laptop computer. College computer labs are readily available and heavily used, but having your own technology is probably a necessity. Some campuses provide laptops as part of the cost of attendance. Others make a laptop purchase easy and inexpensive on campus. Check out the standard procedure at your school. This information will usually be shared at summer orientation and on the college's website. Most students will probably find that they need to have their own laptop with them when they arrive on campus.

Colleges today have increasingly large investments in all kinds of technology. They work hard against big obstacles to support an array of hardware and software needed for teaching, learning, information, and communication. Check with the college's information technology team to see what they expect or require. Likely the laptop you bring with you must be configured with certain minimum capacities to connect to and be supported by the college's technology and staff.

It may take awhile to sort out how to best access campus systems. All computer teams are very busy and stressed at the beginning of a new school year as they try to incorporate so many new people and machines all at once. How well they do their job is another clear signal of the college's commitment to your success.

To be successful in college (and in life), you need to learn how to make informed choices for yourself. For most students, through high school, decisions are shaped by parents and schools. Colleges that produce successful graduates are conscious of helping maturing individuals make their own choices and experience the successes and sometimes failures that result. Your college choice has been among the most important decisions of your life so far. It has prepared you to really begin taking responsibility for shaping your life. You are ready.

MYTHS ABOUT MOVING IN

On move-in day, the father of an entering student was sitting by himself having lunch in the dining hall. He seemed to be quietly talking to himself, almost muttering. A campus official, doing what is expected when spotting a guest alone, asked if it would be OK to join the father for lunch. "Sure," said the dad, who continued to repeat the phrase he had been uttering before. At close range, it became clear that the father was saying something like, "It's really here, it's really here." The official couldn't resist asking what it was that was "really here."

"What's really here," the dad responded, "is what you promised. I kept thinking that when you knew my kid was coming, when finally on campus, that the friendship and support and attention would all go away and it would be as impersonal and cold as when I went to school. But by golly, now that the recruiting's over, you folks are all still the same. It's really here."

It was really there to that dad—the very words a great college admissions and academic team wants to hear to justify the eighteen months of promises they had been making to that student and all other students. Now that's a college worth attending, one where you are going to be successful and graduate on time, forty-five months later.

Myths 70 to 75 take you to the door of your first classroom on day one, year one of the college experience. There will be pitfalls and worries aplenty but nothing you can't handle. Remember that the turtle only makes progress when it sticks its neck out. Be not afraid.

Myth 70: Move-in day is always a nightmare on a college campus.

Reality: Some colleges provide enough cheerful help to make it almost fun.

The day has finally arrived. The station wagon and pickup truck are ready and loaded with old stuff, new purchases, and plywood to build lofts in the dorm room. Mom and Dad have taken the day off. All the preparation is over; this is what you have been working toward. You have a time and place to arrive.

On many campuses, it isn't a lot of fun. Usually move-in is on the hottest August day anyone can remember. Vans are backed up for seven blocks. Elevators stopped working long ago. Ice water is hard to find.

If you shopped right and chose wisely, however, the campus you are arriving at may very well surprise you. The horror stories you have been hearing from high school friends about their experiences may not be yours at all. Traffic and parking can be organized and orderly. Lots of student and staff help may be handy as you unload. Smiling faces will find your keys and direct you to your room. This is college the way it ought to be: welcoming, accessible, and friendly. You have enough difficult transitions to face soon, and they know it and want to make it as easy as possible. Later that day, there will be the first of important start-up meetings, and you need to be ready.

If the move-in is not quite as graceful as you

hope, there are a few things you can do. Let your family and friends do as much of the grunt work as possible. They are nervous too and want to feel useful. Soon, they get back to showers, air conditioning, and life as usual. Keep them busy; you can always rearrange later. Or maybe leave some nonessentials in your car, if you are keeping one on campus, and move them in later or the next day when things calm down. Keep stuff at home you don't absolutely need right away. After you and your roommate figure out what goes where, you will have a better feel anyway for what you really need. No sense dragging something back home that you never used anyway.

One useful trick is to see if you can check into the hall early by a day or two. Returning students will have figured out how to do this. The easiest way is to be part of a team or organization—such as a cross country or football team, a fraternity or sorority, the residence hall, campus technology, or food-service staff—that has to be up and going before the start of school.

By mid-afternoon of student move-in day (usually a week or so before classes start) enough order will be restored that a meeting or two will be held for new students and parents, usually ending in time for parents to leave and students to have their first campus meal together. Good college orientation programs are concerned about smoothly exiting parents from campus, and with good reason.

Myth 71: Families are more than ready for the beginning of college.

Reality: Separation of parents and new students can be difficult or traumatic.

For eighteen months, in fact for eighteen years, parents and their children have been getting ready, knowingly or not, for this moment. There is no other place anyone would rather be. By doing the college search the right way, parents and student have been involved in the decision-making process and feel good about the choice. All concerned will have to make some continuing personal sacrifices to make a college education affordable, but everyone knows it is a great investment in your future.

But still the moment of separation, no matter how much prepared for and visualized, will reach up and grab parents and students emotionally in ways they could not have expected. It seems you are leaving home forever. It will be awhile before the reality sinks in that you will be home for some holidays, long breaks, and summertime. Suddenly, at the moment of move-in-day goodbyes, childhood seems over and adulthood begins.

You have told each other over and over again the things you want to remember. There is nothing left to say, but you will try anyway. No matter what issues might cause conflict between almost-grown-up children and their parents, this moment of departure brings back a flood of memories, mostly good and loving.

The college and each of you can make separation more tolerable. Move-in programming will demand your attention so you will not be able to dawdle over the family leaving. Talented college speakers will have purposely left parents feeling good and on a high about your upcoming experiences. Hopefully, no questions will be left unanswered.

It's up to you to make sure you agree to follow up on communication. Thank goodness for instant messages, text messaging, email, and cell phones. Keep each other in the loop. Have a message of some sort, however brief, waiting for each other tonight—you all know exactly when parents will get home. Good contact is in everyone's best interest. With all the changes ahead, the people who know and love you best and longest will be an amazing support system for each other. Parents will have a zillion questions as they identify with your new life. Try to anticipate some of them so they can depend on you to keep them up-to-date and not feel that they have to hound or interrogate you, which is uncomfortable for all concerned. Parents should keep their student aware of what's going on at home, as well, to minimize homesickness.

One trick that always works and gets you out of the cafeteria is to wait a few days and then pick a time a week or two down the road and invite the family back to town for dinner. A grown-up meal in a nice restaurant will be something everyone looks forward to immensely and will look back upon gratefully. Be ready to share the good as well as the bad and keep the financial requests or surprises to a minimum. Let the family see your room and chat with your roommate. The more everyone understands and relates to the college experience (spare them some of the foolish teenage things that happen in a residence hall or a Saturday night), the more successful the college years will be for all concerned.

Myth 72: Most students don't experience homesickness.

Reality: Feeling really down for a while is a common and sometimes fairly severe problem.

When parents leave, some energetic orientation student leader will whisk you away to a fun activity and meal with lots of other students. No aspect of move-in is more programmed and regimented than this post-separation moment. If a tear welled up in a parent's eye, the natural tendency of the student is to choke up and want to be alone so as not to be embarrassed. Wrong! Get out there and stay out there.

Homesickness has no early warning signs. It just hits like a ton of bricks all at once and can bring everyone to their knees. Most people entering college have never experienced this wave of emotion and separation anxiety before. Feeling alone and isolated is one of life's scarier moments. If you are immune, that's great. But if you are blue, try desperately to lean into the flood of structured fun that campus and student leaders have in store for you.

Stay close to other students. Be active. Get involved. This is the perfect time to dive into that activity you have been thinking about trying. Physical exercise, team sports, community and campus service projects, more placement tests, and scavenger hunts are available and often required in the first few days at college to keep you out of your room and busy.

The first ready responders on campus are the corps of student residence-hall assistants. It still takes courage, but it's easiest to talk one-on-one with a sympathetic fellow student. The resident assistants (RAs) have been brought to campus a week or so before your arrival, and they have been trained to look for and manage your issues. Nothing works better than hearing that this relaxed, confident, comfortable student leader went through just the same experience you are feeling now and to be reassured that it will pass. In fact, when homesickness leaves, it is one of those things that you just cannot remember how bad it felt.

If the RA thinks that you might benefit from more experienced help, you may well be referred to the campus counseling center. Don't feel foolish about going. As a top high school student you probably managed all your tough issues well and feel totally self-reliant. Help was something slower, less-successful students needed, not something you availed yourself of, no matter what.

College is different. The slower students are not here. This is a fast track, and there may be many bumpy spots. A college intent on seeing you successful has a great deal of appropriate and discreet help available for whatever ails your mind, body, or spirit. The counselor will be young and full of life. Just talking once or twice will probably fix everything. You will usually not make or might cancel a third appointment because the need is gone. Just asking for or taking help is probably a signal that you are better already.

Myth 73: Alcohol abuse is only a problem for a minority of students.

Reality: Almost all college students have to confront problems related to alcohol on campus either in themselves or in someone close to them.

Sad to say, but alcohol is a social lubricant and a problem for many Americans. College campuses are no exception, especially when young people experience new-found freedoms, peer social pressure, and parties often built around excessive alcohol availability.

Colleges are careful to identify their policies regarding alcohol. Prior to the uniformity of a twenty-one-year-old legal drinking age, some campuses were "wet," allowing for wide-open drinking. These colleges were trying to prevent students from having to break the rules in order to drink. Now that the great majority of residential undergraduates are not of legal age, colleges cannot condone public drinking. Almost every campus today has rules against open drinking at campus parties and events. Fraternities and sororities are closely monitored, primarily by their alumni leaders, because of the legal and insurance risks of personal and property damage associated with alcohol's effects.

Many campuses allow legal-age students to drink in the privacy of their own rooms. Some are more restrictive and declare themselves "dry," with alcohol allowed nowhere. This is especially true at schools with church relationships that discourage any alcohol use or where colleges have had to react to major problems such as binge drinking that got out of control.

No matter the policy, the facts are that on every campus, students of all ages can find opportunities to drink. Early in the new academic year, often during move-in week, new students will face invitations to parties, usually off campus. Just about every college has to cope with violations of its alcohol policy during these times. Some police their own students, while others allow local authorities to administer the law. Sanctions vary widely from a slap on the wrist to expulsion and jail time. Students learn quickly what they can and can't get away with and what punishments they will face. People who serve alcohol to minors are putting themselves at particular risk for severe penalties.

Some colleges will get parents involved in hopes of getting help from home. Others will protect student privacy in most cases. Perhaps toughest for students are alcohol problems they know about involving friends, roommates, and fraternity/ sorority brothers and sisters. Most of the time, there is social pressure not to report a peer. Often, however, it is a necessity for the other person's well-being, difficult as it may be to point the finger.

There are times when you will not be able to sleep or study because of the raucous environment surrounding alcohol use or the discomfort of its aftermath on the condition of your room or residence hall. No one enjoys getting up on a weekend morning to a pretty campus littered with empty beer bottles everywhere.

Campus and student leaders will try to turn alcohol excess into a learning opportunity for all concerned. If someone who has a problem gets help with it before it really gets out of hand and threatens success, health, or life itself, then all concerned will be the better for it.

Myth 74: There is not any one special skill that all students must master for college success.

Reality: Time management must be learned, practiced, and mastered.

A successful business person and college alumnus, twenty years beyond graduation, returned to his alma mater to address a class of senior business majors. The first thing he did in front of the group was to take a pocket calendar out and ask students which of them carried something like this to keep track of their schedules. About half the audience said they did.

The alum was very direct. He said, "Look around. These folks with the calendars will be the successful ones in this group. Time is one thing we all have the same amount of and can't buy anymore. How we manage it is what really matters. The richest people in the world and the homeless guy in the street have exactly the same amount. Look at how differently they use it."

Time management must be learned early in the college years. So, you might as well go to one of the seminars about it offered on your campus during the first few days of school. Get a calendar. There are many options, both paper and electronic. Any system that works for you is fine. Just make sure you use it.

The issue of time is especially important for a new college student. Even successful people in high school pretty much operated with a tight schedule of class after class throughout the day, and probably had people at home reminding them of what needed to be done. A residential college is a 24/7 world. Even if you attend a "suitcase" campus and go home every weekend, there are still many, many more hours in the week that you will not be in class. Each student schedule is different, and there is nobody around to prompt you about what happens next.

It seems like there is so much time that wasting a few hours here and there doesn't matter. Downtime is important to build into a busy schedule, but wasting time can become a habit. The academic pace flies by, and soon tests and papers will be on top of you. Having lots of activities and responsibilities sounds like it would be more stressful, but usually a busy person is an organized person.

Figure out when and how you study best. Get your work done a little at a time and on schedule. Professors won't constantly remind you of what is due, but they will give you a class outline called a syllabus at the beginning of the term, and you can block out how you are going to get it all done.

Manage your schedule; don't let it manage you. Make keeping track of your time and obligations reduce rather than add to your stress levels. Check your plan every so often and modify whatever needs to be changed. Write down everything you have to do and find a place in the time schedule where you know it can and will be done.

Ask students who you admire how they get everything done. Bend their ways to fit your personality.

One tip that will come in handy from a highly successful student is to make appointments with yourself or your bed for sleep. College students stay up very late. It's just a part of the culture. Very few students eat breakfast in the cafeteria. Campuses come awake slowly, and sometimes not at all, on Saturday mornings. Schedule an hour or two for a power nap. That will be time well spent on your road to success and graduation.

Myth 75: There is no way to predict on the first morning of college who the successful graduates will be.

Reality: How a student has selected and prepared for this day probably determines how successful the experience ahead will be.

One pundit likes to say that the secret to life is "showing up, dressed and ready to play." Attendance may not even be taken in many of your college classes, but it makes sense to be there. After all, you or someone is paying for the experience, and you might as well get some return on the investment.

If possible, study the college's internal website for information before attending your first classes. Most faculty now post their class outlines online. You, and the instructor, will be impressed if you have gotten a bit ahead on the reading and other early class assignments. Most importantly, you will feel confident and ready for whatever surprises come your way. The beginning of school is exciting and a bit scary. You will likely believe that all the other students are smarter and better prepared for college than you are. In reality, everyone else feels that way about you. Just relax and settle in. The pace of classes will be faster than you have experience before, and you will be expected to learn independently. But you do have a bit of time to lean into the experienced and congratulate yourself on being in the right place.

* * *

Final Thoughts

You have gone about the college search and preparation in a proactive fashion. You didn't let yourself get bumped about, being controlled or powerlessly victimized by a nameless, faceless college process.

Every step of the way, you were aware that you had choices and deserved to be treated with the same respect that you were willing to show to others. You have looked inward to know yourself better. The things you value, respect, and admire that shape your identity have had an impact on finding the right college for you. It may be big or small, tax supported or church related, urban or rural, single-sex or coeducational, but it's your college and you know why.

You may be playing on a team or in the band, joining a Greek organization or living in a theme house, but in each case you have chosen to do what you can best learn from and how you can be most successful.

College is probably costing you and your family a good bit of money, and all concerned are making sacrifices, but you know that you have shopped wisely and have gotten all the financial aid available and appropriate. The investment in your future is manageable and wise.

Know that for all your advance work, you are here to learn. And that means there will be mistakes, false starts, and rocky spots en route to graduation day. Look upon these moments, much as you will dislike them, as chances to break new ground, figure out how to cope and grow, and get stronger for it. If you knew everything there was to know, you wouldn't need to be in college. Learning is fun, but it is also hard work and sometimes scary as you challenge old, safe assumptions.

In the next few years, you will learn such things as how to speak someone else's language, how scientists discover truths about our amazing world, how Iago challenged Othello's devotion to Desdemona, how the Federal Constitution was ratified, how to dance the salsa, and thousands of other things. You will get so much better at reading, writing, and speaking. You will become comfortable with quantitative and technological problem solving, and you will build permanent friendships.

It is the time of your life, and you are more than ready. Go for it. Be successful. Graduate!

INDEX

G

gender 28, 37–39, 67, 113, 117
goal
    college's 64
    target 85
    ultimate 93
government
    agencies 150
    federal 146, 163, 175
    program 150
graduate
    assistants 102
    program 104
    programs, excellent 103
graduation
    day 231
    rates 74, 185
    rate question 75
grants
    extracurricular 141
    private 155–56
Greek
    campuses 206
    life 92, 208
    organizations 206, 230
    system 205, 207

guide
    books 42–44
    ranking 43

H

high school
    athletes 202
    career 17
    counselors 8–9, 111, 136
    guidance 9
High-achieving students in ACT states 15
homesickness 59, 219–21
Honors colleges 194
housing and food options 171

I

Iago 231
incentives 28, 31, 94
    financial 167

V

validation, independent 43
veteran students 164, 193
visit campus 35, 51–53, 60,
    74, 86, 94, 115
visitation policies 40
volunteer 68

W

websites 38, 48
    college's 211

ABOUT THE AUTHOR

Dr. Jerry Israel has experienced American college life for the past half-century as student, scholar, instructor, dean, president, and now consultant. As an entering student at New York University in the late 1950s, he remembers the opening convocation remarks of the NYU president were to be aware that in college you didn't "take classes, you studied subjects."

Trained as a research historian of American foreign policy in the cataclysmic campus era of the Vietnam War, Dr. Israel redirected his career from scholarship to teaching and assisting students during a fourteen-year stint on the faculty of

Illinois Wesleyan University. Israel believes that his engagement with IWU students as associate academic dean in the 1980s was central to his understanding and commitment to engaged, involved, active student learning.

His presidencies at Morningside College and the University of Indianapolis were characterized by a passion for high-quality service to students in all phases of campus life.

Jerry and Carol Israel (an accomplished K–12 teacher, administrator, and consultant) have three children, all college graduates, and five grandchildren, including a college junior and freshman in the fall of 2008. They live in southwest Florida and both maintain active consulting engagements following retirement from full-time administrative duties in 2005.